VEGETARIAN COOKING IN THE MICROWAVE

SONIA ALLISON
VICTORIA LLOYD-DAVIES

BELL & HYMAN

First published 1986 by
Bell & Hyman Limited
Denmark House
37-39 Queen Elizabeth Street
London SE1 2QB

Designed by Neil Sayer
Illustrations by Paul Saunders
Recipes developed and tested by Victoria Lloyd Davies and
Wendy Dines in a Creda Micro-Plus Microwave

British Library Cataloguing in Publication Data
Allison, Sonia
　　Vegetarian cooking in the microwave
　　1. Vegetarian cookery　2. Microwave cookery
　　I. Title　II. Lloyd-Davies, Victoria
　　641.5'636　　TX837

ISBN 0 7135 2649 1

Typeset by Typecast Ltd., Maidstone
Printed in Great Britain at the University Press, Cambridge

CONTENTS

ACKNOWLEDGEMENTS 4
INTRODUCTION 5
SOUPS 9
GRAINS, BEANS AND PULSES 19
NUTS 37
RICE AND PASTA 49
EGGS AND CHEESE 65
VEGETABLES 77
SAUCES 113
BREADS AND CAKES 127
FRUITS AND PUDDINGS 149
PRESERVES 167
DRINKS 177
MISCELLANEOUS 185
INDEX 188

ACKNOWLEDGEMENTS

The authors and publishers would like to thank the following organisations for sponsoring photographs for the book. The Apple and Pear Development Council facing pages 33 below, 97, in collaboration with Ocean Spray Cranberry Sauces facing page 161; Baxters of Speyside facing page 49; British Alcan Consumer Products Limited facing pages 49 below, 80 above, 96, 128. The California Raisin Advisory Board facing pages 48, 129; Corning Microwave Cookware Collection facing pages 81, 144; TI Creda Limited facing pages 176, 177; The English Country Cheese Council facing page 80; The Flour Advisory Bureau facing pages 145, 160; Kellogg Company of Great Britain Limited facing page 97 above; Modern Health Products Limited, manufacturers of Vecon facing page 33 above; The Mushroom Growers' Association facing page 32; Ocean Spray Cranberry Sauces with the Apple and Pear Development Council facing page 161;

In addition they wish to thank Wendy Dines who developed and tested the recipes with Victoria Lloyd Davies; Diane Freedman, Trisha Payne and Helen Wildbore who helped her with several recipes; Jenny Barber who typed the manuscript; and her family Fred, Jessica and Lucy Silvester who tasted and gave their opinions on the recipes; the photographers Barry Bullough, David Cave, Melvin Gray and Roy Rich; and the artist Paul Saunders.

4

_INTRODUCTION

This book is a successful partnership between two very popular present-day trends; microwave cooking and vegetarianism. The recipes themselves, all of which have been thoroughly tested in home-based kitchens, are delicious, reliable and well-suited to the creation of personalised menu-making while the choice of dishes is surprisingly wide-ranging and covers soups, grains, beans, pulses, nuts, rice, pasta, eggs, cheese, vegetables, sauces, breads, cakes, fruits, puddings, preserves and drinks.

Vegetarians will welcome the speed with which the food cooks in the microwave; the way flavour, colour and food nutrients are retained; the overall economy of fuel; the high saving in effort. The considerable advantages of microwave cooking are well-known to experienced users but for those still unfamiliar with the techniques, the guide below should prove helpful.

Understanding Microwaves
Microwaves, based on radar, have been used in cooking appliances for over 40 years and are a form of electro-magnetic energy consisting of short-length, non-ionising and high frequency radio waves at the top end of the radio band. They are near to infra-red rays but not as powerful.

How Microwaves Work In An Oven
In a microwave oven, microwaves are emitted from a device known as a magnetron, usually situated at the top of the oven and placed to one side. They are transmitted into the oven cavity down a channel known as a waveguide then bounce from side to side like a ball. They then beam on to the food from all directions and cause the liquid within the food itself to vibrate so fast that rapid friction is set up which creates enough

5

heat to cook the food cleanly, rapidly and effectively.

Microwave Distribution
To ensure even cooking, most models are fitted with a concealed stirrer fan situated at the top or base of the oven. This rotates while the oven is switched on and helps to distribute the microwaves. The turntables in some models also assist in making sure the waves reach every part of the food.

Shape of Dishes
Because microwaves are able only to penetrate 1in (2.5cm) of the food from top to bottom and side to side, shallow dishes for cooking are recommended unless the recipe states otherwise. Round dishes give the best results, followed by oval. Food in square or oblong dishes sometimes cooks unevenly at the corners.

How To Arrange Food
To allow the microwaves maximum penetration, thick pieces of food should be placed towards the outside of the plate or dish, leaving the centre as empty as possible. For example, 3 potatoes or apples etc should be arranged in a triangle, 4 in a square, 6 to 8 in a ring. Food should *never* be piled up as cooking will be noticeably uneven. Stirring some of the dishes during and at the end of cooking helps to distribute heat but this should take place only where recommended in the recipe.

Standing Or Resting Times
To enable heat to transfer itself from the outside edges to the centre and ensure even cooking, some dishes should be left to stand half way through their cooking cycle and/or at the end. Individual recipes will specify.

Warning
Never switch on an empty oven or the magnetron may be damaged.

Cleaning

Wipe out the oven cavity with a clean, damp dishcloth then dry with a tea towel. Alternatively, remove stubborn stains with a nail brush dipped in detergent water then rinse off.

Choice Of Crockery

Crockery chosen should be made of materials through which microwaves can pass directly to the food in the same way as sunlight passes through a window pane. These include all the ranges of plastic microware currently on the market from Anchor Hocking, Thorpac, Lakeland Plastics, Bejam and other leading manufacturers; different types of crockery glass (but not crystal), and glass ceramic cookware such as Corningware and Pyrex; roasting or boiling bags, cling film (also known as plastic wrap) from British Alcan; basketware, paper and wood. Metal containers should NEVER be used as they reflect microwaves away from the food and prevent it from cooking. Similarly, crockery with silver and gold trims should not be used as they can have a damaging effect on the magnetron and also on themselves. Although most utensils remain relatively cool to the touch, some absorb a surprising amount of heat from the food. Thus, to prevent discomfort, dishes should be removed from the microwave with hands protected by oven gloves.

Browning Dish

This is a ceramic dish, its base coated with special tin oxide material. It becomes extremely hot when pre-heated and is useful for searing or 'frying' food prior to cooking. The food browns on the outside and looks as if cooked by conventional grilling or frying. The dish is always pre-heated while empty for about 5 minutes though this varies according to the food being cooked. Be guided by the recipes or instruction book accompanying the browning dish. It is important to note that every time a batch of food has been cooked, the dish will need cleaning and pre-heating for half the length of time required initially. Although the dish yellows while in use, it returns to its old colour when cold.

Temperature Probe
This registers the internal temperature of joints of meat etc as an indication of whether they are done.

Power Controls
In general, microwave ovens vary between 500 and 700 watt outputs with corresponding inputs of 1000 and 1500 watts. Recipes in this book have been prepared in a Creda Micro-Plus oven with a 600 watt output and the following variable power settings:

600 watts	FULL POWER	(100% power)
500 watts	REHEAT	(83% power)
400 watts	ROAST	(67% power)
325 watts	SIMMER	(54% power)
230 watts	DEFROST	(38% power)
100 watts	WARM	(17% power)

Cooking times have been given for a 600 watt oven.
For a 500 watt oven *increase* timing by approximately 25 seconds for each minute.
For a 700 watt oven *decrease* timing by approximately 25 seconds for each minute.

Note

The quantities for recipes in this book are given in imperial and metric measurements. It is important not to mix these measurements in any given recipe as they are proportionate.

Flour
In late 1986 the names of certain flours will be altered. Wholewheat flour will become wholemeal. 85% wheatmeal will become 85% brown. 81% wheatmeal will become 81% brown. Granary will become malted brown flour.

SOUPS

Soups are a pleasure to make in the microwave
and most require only one bowl. And the speed is
a wonder: Split Pea in 15 minutes, Minestrone in
just over 20, Mushroom in 8. All nutritive value is
retained, colours are bright, and flavours full and
rounded. There is no danger of any soup catching
on the bottom of the bowl but to save soiling the
oven, the bowl should be put on to a plate in case
the liquid boils over.

Split Pea Soup

8oz (225g) split peas, covered with boiling water and left to soak for 1 hour

6oz (175g) onion, chopped

6oz (175g) potato, thickly sliced

2 cloves garlic, crushed

1½ tsp vegetable stock extract

2pt (1.2l) boiling water

sea salt and freshly-milled black pepper to taste

To garnish

¼pt (150ml) single cream

sprigs of fresh mint

A quick, economical and fulfilling soup, delicious with granary rolls or wedges of brown toast.

1. Drain split peas then place in a 4pt (2.25l) glass or pottery bowl with vegetables and garlic.
2. Mix vegetable stock extract and boiling water together. Pour over vegetables.
3. Cover dish with cling film and puncture twice with the tip of a knife. Place on a plate in case the water boils over.
4. Cook on FULL POWER for 15 minutes. Keep covered and leave to stand for 10 minutes.
5. Pour, in 2 or 3 batches, into a blender goblet and blend until smooth.
6. Add seasoning then return to rinsed-out dish. Re-cover as before and cook on REHEAT for 2 minutes until hot.
7. Garnish each helping with a swirl of cream and a sprig of fresh mint.

Leek with Corn Soup

Serves 6

1oz (25g) vegetable fat

8oz (225g) trimmed leeks, thoroughly washed and finely-chopped

1 level tblsp whole grain mustard

7oz (200g) frozen sweetcorn kernels

1½ level tsp vegetable stock extract

A subtle hint of lemon complements the more pronounced flavour of the leeks in this creamy and elegant soup. Accompany with rye bread.

1. Place vegetable fat in a 3½pt (2l) glass or pottery dish with leeks. Cover with cling film, puncture twice with the tip of a knife.
2. Cook on FULL POWER for 3 minutes.
3. Stir in mustard and sweetcorn.

1¾pt (1l) boiling water

1 level tblsp cornflour

2 level tblsp lemon juice

sea salt and freshly-milled
black pepper to taste

To garnish

chopped parsley

Serves 4

2 tblsp rape seed oil

3oz (75g) onion, finely
chopped

1lb (450g) carrots, peeled and
finely chopped

½ level tsp vegetable stock
extract

1pt (600ml) boiling water

1 level tsp sugar

2 level tsp coriander seeds,
crushed

sea salt and freshly-milled
black pepper to taste

2 level tblsp chopped parsley

¼pt (150ml) single cream

4. Mix vegetable stock extract with boiling water and pour over vegetables.

5. Blend cornflour with lemon juice until smooth, then stir into dish.

6. Cover with a plate and cook on FULL POWER for 6 minutes, stirring 3 times during cooking.

7. Add seasoning. Sprinkle each helping with parsley before serving.

Carrot and Coriander Soup

A light, refreshing soup which retains its splendid natural colour when cooked in the microwave.

1. Place rape seed oil in a 3½pt (2l) glass or pottery casserole. Add onion and fry on FULL POWER FOR 3 minutes. Leave uncovered.

2. Add carrots and cook on FULL POWER for a further 2 minutes.

3. Dissolve vegetable stock extract in boiling water and add to carrot and onion with the sugar, coriander seeds and seasoning to taste. Cover with cling film then puncture twice with the tip of a knife.

4. Cook on FULL POWER for 12 minutes until the vegetables are tender. Leave to stand for 5 minutes.

5. Purée mixture, in 2 or 3 batches, in a blender or food processor. Return to rinsed-out bowl, cover with a plate and cook on FULL POWER for 5 minutes or until heated through. Stir twice.

6. Just before serving, adjust seasoning and stir in parsley and cream.

11

Lentil and Cheese Soup

Serves 6

2 tblsp rape seed oil

6oz (175g) onion, finely chopped

4oz (125g) carrots, peeled and finely chopped

8oz (225g) red lentils

2pt (1.2l) boiling water

4oz (125g) Red Leicestershire cheese, grated

sea salt and freshly-milled black pepper to taste

A tasty soup for cold days which needs a food processor or blender goblet for smoothness. Serve it with wholewheat scones, or even fruity ones.

1. Put oil into a 3½pt (2l) glass or pottery bowl. Add the finely chopped onion, carrots, and red lentils. Stir well. Cover with cling film then puncture twice with the tip of a knife. Place on a plate in case water boils over. Cook for 5 minutes on FULL POWER.
2. Remove from microwave, mix in boiling water and re-cover as before. Cook on FULL POWER for 5 minutes.
3. Reduce to SIMMER and cook for a further 25 minutes.
4. Leave to stand for 10 minutes then blend until smooth in food processor or blender goblet. Return soup to rinsed-out bowl.
5. Add cheese and stir with a wooden spoon until melted. Season to taste and serve.

Beetroot and Orange Soup

Serves 6-8

1oz (25g) vegetable fat

4oz (125g) carrots, cut into 1½in (4cm) long matchsticks

2 sticks celery, thinly sliced

6oz (175g) onion, finely chopped

2 cloves garlic, crushed

A vividly bright soup with a sophisticated flavour. It may be served steaming hot or well-chilled.

1. Place vegetable fat in a 4pt (2.25l) glass or pottery dish with carrots, celery, onion and garlic. Cover with cling film, puncture twice with the tip of a knife.

8oz (225g) fresh tomatoes
peeled and finely chopped

2 level tblsp chopped parsley

8oz (225g) cooked beetroot,
finely chopped

grated rind and juice of 1
large orange

1½ level tsp vegetable stock
extract

2½pt (1.5l) boiling water

sea salt and freshly-milled
black pepper to taste

¼pt (150ml) soured cream

2. Cook on FULL POWER for 3 minutes.
3. Stir in tomatoes, parsley, beetroot and orange rind.
4. Mix vegetable stock extract with boiling water. Pour over vegetables.
5. Re-cover then cook on FULL POWER for 7 minutes.
6. Stir in orange juice and seasoning.
7. Serve with a bowl of soured cream handed separately.

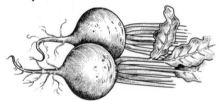

Serves 4

2 tblsp rape seed oil

3oz (75g) onion, peeled and
finely chopped

8oz (225g) flat mushrooms,
wiped clean and chopped

1½ level tsp vegetable stock
extract

2pt (1.2l) boiling water

grated rind of ½ lemon

4oz (125g) fresh wholemeal
breadcrumbs

sea salt and freshly-milled
black pepper to taste

2 rounded tblsp soured cream

Mushroom Soup

A traditional, nourishing soup thickened with brown breadcrumbs instead of flour.

1. Place oil, onion and mushrooms into a 3½pt (2l) glass or pottery dish. Cover with cling film, then puncture twice with the tip of a knife.
2. Cook on FULL POWER for 3 minutes.
3. Dissolve vegetable stock extract in boiling water and add to mushrooms with lemon rind, breadcrumbs and seasoning.
4. Cook on REHEAT for 5 minutes. Stir in soured cream and sprinkle with parsley.

Cucumber and Watercress Soup

Serves 4

2 bunches of watercress, washed

6oz (150g) onion, coarsely chopped

grated rind of 2 lemons

1pt (600ml) boiling water

3oz (75g) ground almonds

½ cucumber, peeled and very finely diced

¼pt (150ml) single low fat cream

1½ level tsp sea salt

A refreshing chilled soup, ideal for warm summer evenings.

1. Put watercress, onion, lemon rind and boiling water in a 3pt (1.75l) glass or pottery bowl. Cover with cling film and puncture twice with the tip of a knife. Cook on FULL POWER for 15 minutes.

2. Remove from the oven and blend mixture until smooth in a food processor or blender. Return to the bowl and stir in ground almonds, cucumber, cream and salt. Transfer to a 2½pt (1.5l) serving bowl. Cover.

3. Chill in a refrigerator and serve with wholemeal rolls.

Sweet Potato Soup

Serves 4

2 tblsp rape seed oil

1lb (450g) sweet potatoes, peeled and sliced

½oz (15g) chopped fresh ginger

1 level tsp vegetable stock extract

1½pt (900ml) boiling water

sea salt and freshly-milled black pepper to taste

¼pt (150ml) single cream

An unusual winter vegetable converts into a spicy, rich soup which goes well with home-baked or shop-bought cheese straws.

1. Place oil, sweet potatoes and chopped ginger into a 3½pt (2l) glass or pottery dish. Cover with cling film then puncture twice with the tip of a knife.

2. Cook on FULL POWER for 7 minutes, lifting cling film and stirring twice during the cooking period.

3. Dissolve vegetable stock extract in boiling water and add to sweet potatoes with the seasoning to taste. Re-cover as above.

4. Cook on FULL POWER for 5 minutes, then purée in a blender or food processor.

5. Return to microwave and REHEAT, covered as before, for 5 minutes.

6. Stir in cream and serve.

Chilled Lettuce and Cucumber Soup

Serves 6

1 small lettuce, washed

½ large cucumber, wiped and chopped into ½in (1.25cm) cubes

3oz (75g) potato, peeled and chopped into ½in (1.25cm) cubes

3oz (75g) onion, peeled and chopped into ½in (1.25cm) pieces

few sprigs parsley

juice of one small lemon

1pt (600ml) boiling water

1 level tsp vegetable stock extract

sea salt and freshly-milled black pepper to taste

1pt (600ml) cold water

To garnish

1 lemon, sliced

A marvellously relaxing icy soup for hot summer evenings. It keeps well in the refrigerator for two to three days and is speedy to prepare.

1. Place all the ingredients in a 3½pt (2l) glass mixing bowl. Cover with cling film and puncture twice with the tip of a knife. Cook on FULL POWER for 5 minutes.

2. Remove from microwave and stir well with a wooden spoon. Re-cover as above, return to microwave and cook on FULL POWER for a further 5 minutes.

3. Once again, stir well and cook on FULL POWER for a further 5 minutes.

4. Cool then blend until smooth in food processor or blender.

5. Season to taste and stir in cold water.

6. Cover and chill until required.

7. Serve each helping garnished with sliced lemon.

Red Lentil and Tomato Soup

Serves 6

8oz (225g) split red lentils

1oz (25g) vegetable fat

6oz (175g) onion, chopped

12oz (350g) fresh tomatoes, peeled and chopped

2 bay leaves

1½ tsp vegetable stock extract

1¾pt (1l) boiling water

2 level tblsp tamari

sea salt and freshly-milled black pepper to taste

To garnish

6 tblsp chopped parsley

A quick-to-make, tasty and colourful soup which teams perfectly with triangles of brown toast or sesame seed bread. Tamari is a wheat-free sauce, slightly thicker and stronger than the traditional soy sauce.

1. Place lentils in a 4pt (2.25l) glass or pottery dish. Add sufficient boiling water to come ½in (1.25cm) over the top. Cover with cling film and puncture twice with the tip of a knife. Place on a plate in case water boils over.
2. Cook on FULL POWER for 5 minutes. Keep covered and leave to stand for 10 minutes.
3. Place vegetable fat in a small glass or pottery dish with the onion. Cover as before and cook on FULL POWER for 3 minutes.
4. Drain lentils and return to dish. Stir in cooked onion, tomatoes and bay leaves.
5. Mix vegetable stock extract with boiling water and pour over lentils.
6. Cover with cling film and puncture twice with the tip of a knife, place dish on a plate and cook on FULL POWER for 4 minutes.
7. Remove bay leaves. Pour mixture, in 2 or 3 batches, into a blender goblet and blend until smooth.
8. Return to rinsed-out dish and stir in tamari and seasoning. Re-cover and cook on REHEAT for 2 minutes until heated through.
9. Sprinkle each helping with chopped parsley.

Minestrone Soup

2oz (50g) haricot beans, covered with boiling water and left to soak for 4 hours

3oz (75g) wholewheat macaroni

8oz (225g) blanched tomatoes, peeled and finely chopped

6oz (175g) carrots, diced

4oz (125g) parsnips, diced

3oz (75g) green pepper, seeds removed and cut into ½in (1.25cm) squares.

3 bay leaves

1½ level tsp vegetable stock extract

2pt (1.25l) boiling water

1oz (25g) vegetable fat

4oz (125g) trimmed leeks, thoroughly washed and finely chopped

4oz (125g) button mushrooms, wiped clean and sliced

sea salt and freshly-milled black pepper to taste

To serve

3 tblsp chopped parsley

2oz (50g) Parmesan cheese, grated

A warming Italian soup laced with haricot beans and wholewheat macaroni. Serve with small dishes of chopped parsley and freshly-grated Parmesan cheese for sprinkling over the top of each helping.

1. Drain haricot beans, then place in a 4pt (2.25l) glass or pottery dish. Pour in sufficient boiling water to come ½in (1.25cm) over the top. Cover with cling film and puncture top twice with the tip of a knife.
2. Cook on FULL POWER for 5 minutes.
3. Drain beans then stir in macaroni, tomatoes, carrots, parsnips, green pepper and bay leaves.
4. Mix vegetable stock extract with boiling water then pour over the vegetables.
5. Re-cover. Cook on FULL POWER for 5 minutes.
6. Stir, re-cover and leave to stand for 8 minutes.
7. Place vegetable fat in a 2pt (1.2l) glass or pottery dish with the leeks and mushrooms. Cover with a plate and cook on FULL POWER for 4 minutes, stirring half way through cooking.
8. Remove bay leaves from Minestrone then stir in leeks, mushrooms and seasoning.
9. Serve with parsley and Parmesan cheese, handed separately.

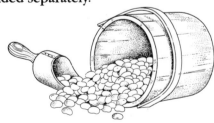

Serves 6

4oz (125g) onion, finely
chopped

1 tblsp rape seed oil

1 level tsp vegetable stock
extract

1½pt (900ml) boiling water

1lb (450g) Jerusalem
artichokes

1 egg yolk, grade 3

¼pt (150ml) soured cream

sea salt and freshly-milled
black pepper to taste

¼ level tsp freshly-grated
nutmeg

2 tblsp scissor-snipped chives

Jerusalem Artichoke Soup with Nutmeg

An elegant cream soup made with a well-loved winter vegetable.

1. Fry the onion in the oil in a shallow glass or pottery dish on FULL POWER for 3 minutes.

2. Dissolve vegetable stock extract in the boiling water and pour 1pt (600ml) into a 3½pt (2l) glass bowl. Peel and thinly slice artichokes into the bowl. Add fried onion.

3. Cover with cling film, then puncture twice with the tip of a knife. Cook on FULL POWER for 15 minutes.

4. Blend artichoke mixture to a smooth purée in a blender or food processor then return to rinsed-out bowl. Stir in remaining stock, egg yolk and soured cream.

5. Cook on REHEAT for 3 minutes, stirring 3 times with a wooden spoon. REHEAT for a further 3 minutes but do not allow to boil as soup will curdle.

6. Check seasoning, then stir in nutmeg. Serve each helping sprinkled with snipped chives.

GRAINS, BEANS AND PULSES

Whether it's a simple bowl of porridge or something more innovative such as Green Pea Rissoles or Red Bean Curry, all dishes based on grains, beans and pulses can be made successfully in the microwave and the overall cooking time is considerably reduced against conventional methods. To encourage the speedy microwaving of beans and pulses, they should be pre-soaked for several hours or overnight and this has been indicated in the recipes where appropriate.

Serves 6

4oz (125g) split red lentils

2 bay leaves

boiling water

½oz (15g) vegetable fat

4oz (125g) onion, grated

8oz (225g) Bramley apples, peeled, cored and finely-chopped

1 level tblsp tahini

sea salt and freshly-milled black pepper to taste

To garnish

1½ level tsp sesame seeds

1 carton or box of mustard and cress

Red Lentil and Apple Pâté

An ideal first course for a celebration meal. The best accompaniment is melba toast.

1. Place lentils and bay leaves in a 2pt (1.25l) glass or pottery dish. Add sufficient boiling water to come ½in (1cm) over the top. Cover with cling film, puncture twice with the tip of a knife. Stand on a plate in case water boils over.

2. Cook on FULL POWER for 5 minutes. Keep covered and leave to stand for 10 minutes.

3. Place vegetable fat in a 1pt (600ml) glass or pottery dish with onion and apples. Cover as above then cook on FULL POWER for 5 minutes, lifting film and stirring half way through cooking time.

4. Remove bay leaves from the lentils and discard. Drain lentils and lightly mash with a fork.

5. Lightly mash apple mixture. Stir into lentils with tahini and seasoning. Mix well. Place into 6 glass or pottery ramekin dishes. Cover and refrigerate until firm.

6. Sprinkle with sesame seeds and garnish with mustard and cress before serving.

Serves 1

2 level tblsp porridge oats

pinch of sea salt

¼pt (150ml) water or skimmed milk

Porridge

1. Put the porridge oats into a 1¾pt (1l) glass or pottery bowl.

2. Add the salt.

3. Pour in the water or skimmed milk and stir well.

4. Cook, uncovered, on FULL POWER until the porridge thickens; approximately 1½ minutes. Stir at the end of every 30 seconds.

5. Serve with milk, sugar or golden syrup.

For 2 portions in 2 bowls

Cook, uncovered, on FULL POWER for 3-3½ minutes.

For 3 portions in 3 bowls

Cook, uncovered, on FULL POWER for 3½-4 minutes.

For 4 portions in 4 bowls

Cook, uncovered, on FULL POWER for 4-4½ minutes.

Lentil Salad

Serves 4

1½ level tsp vegetable stock extract

3pt (1.7l) boiling water

8oz (225g) green lentils

2 medium sticks celery

3oz (75g) green pepper

2 level tblsp chopped parsley

4 tblsp olive oil

2½ tblsp raspberry vinegar

sea salt and freshly-milled black pepper to taste

A very substantial and nourishing salad.

1. Dissolve vegetable stock extract in boiling water and pour over lentils in a 3½pt (2l) glass or pottery dish. Cover with cling film, then puncture twice with the tip of a knife. Stand on a plate in case the water boils over.

2. Cook on FULL POWER for 20 minutes. Leave to stand for 5 minutes. Drain and cool.

3. Add celery, pepper and parsley. Mix well.

4. Whisk remaining ingredients together, then pour dressing over the lentil mixture. Fork-stir well to mix.

5. Cover and lightly chill before serving.

Chilli Lentil and Mushroom Pie

Serves 4-6

12oz (350g) potatoes, peeled and diced

12oz (350g) swede, peeled and diced

3 tblsp water

8oz (225g) split red lentils

boiling water

2oz (50g) vegetable fat

3 fresh green chilli peppers, seeds removed and finely sliced

1 medium onion, peeled and chopped

6oz (175g) flat mushrooms, wiped clean and finely chopped

1 level tsp vegetable stock extract

7oz (200g) cooked sweetcorn kernels, drained

14oz (400g) can tomatoes, drained and chopped

sea salt and freshly-milled black pepper

A colourful vegetable mixture flavoured with fresh chilli peppers and topped with creamy potato and swede. Simply serve a green vegetable to complete the meal.

1. Place potatoes and swede in a glass basin with water. Cover with a plate then cook on FULL POWER for 14 minutes, stirring with a wooden spoon after 7 minutes. Keep covered and leave to stand while continuing with rest of preparations.

2. Place lentils in a 3½pt (2l) glass or pottery dish. Add sufficient boiling water to come ½in (1.25cm) over the top. Cover with cling film and puncture twice with the tip of a knife. Stand on a plate in case the water boils over.

3. Cook on FULL POWER for 6 minutes then keep covered and leave to stand for 10 minutes.

4. Place 1oz (25g) vegetable fat in a small glass or pottery dish with chillies, onion and mushrooms. Cover with a plate then cook on FULL POWER for 3 minutes.

5. Drain off excess water from the lentils and stir in cooked vegetables, vegetable stock extract, sweetcorn, tomatoes and seasoning. Mix well with a wooden spoon.

6. Mash potatoes and swede with remaining vegetable fat until fluffy. Season, then use to cover the other vegetables.

7. Cook on REHEAT for 6 minutes. (If liked, the topping may be browned under a hot grill.)

Crunchy Lentil Balls

Serves 4-6

8oz (225g) brown lentils, covered with boiling water and left to soak for an hour

boiling water

1oz (25g) vegetable fat

2 medium leeks, washed and finely chopped

2 cloves garlic, peeled and crushed

4oz (125g) flat mushrooms, wiped clean and finely chopped

3oz (75g) green pepper, seeds removed and finely chopped

1 level tsp ground turmeric

1 level tsp ground cumin

2 level tsp ground coriander

sea salt and freshly-milled black pepper to taste

3oz (75g) brown rice flour

a little wholewheat flour

To coat

2 grade 3 eggs, beaten

4oz (125) crushed wheat flakes, placed in a plastic bag

Well-flavoured and appetising, the balls should be accompanied by gravy, creamed potatoes and cauliflower.

1. Drain lentils, then place in a 2pt (1.25l) glass dish. Add sufficient boiling water to come ½in (1.25cm) over the top.
2. Cover with cling film then puncture twice with the tip of a knife. Cook on FULL POWER for 10 minutes. Keep covered and leave to stand for a further 10 minutes.
3. Place vegetable fat, leeks, garlic, mushrooms and green pepper into a glass or pottery dish and cover with a plate. Cook on FULL POWER for 2 minutes.
4. Stir in spices and seasoning, re-cover then cook on FULL POWER for a further 1 minute.
5. Drain off any excess water from the lentils, then stir in the vegetables and brown rice flour.
6. When completely cold, shape into 12 balls with well-floured hands. Dip each in beaten egg, pop into the plastic bag and gently shake until well-coated with wheat flakes.
7. Cook on FULL POWER on a pre-heated browning dish for 3 minutes each side.

Tip
Lentil Balls are a little messy when shaping into balls, so use plenty of wholewheat flour on your hands.

Serves 6-8

4oz (125g) couscous

1½oz (40g) vegetable fat

6oz (175g) onion, chopped

2oz (50g) carrots, thinly
sliced

4oz (125g) white cabbage,
finely shredded

4oz (125g) frozen peas

4oz (125g) bulgar wheat

1pt (600ml) boiling water

sea salt and freshly-milled
black pepper to taste

Couscous with Bulgar Wheat

This is a versatile dish, just as tasty cold as hot and therefore an excellent choice for a buffet party or picnic.

1. Moisten couscous with warm water to cover and leave aside for 10 minutes.
2. Place vegetable fat in a large glass or pottery mixing bowl with onion, carrots and cabbage. Cover with a plate then cook on FULL POWER for 7 minutes, stirring twice during cooking.
3. Mix in peas, re-cover and leave on one side temporarily.
4. Drain couscous then turn into a 3½pt (2l) glass or pottery dish. Stir in bulgar wheat and boiling water. Cover with a matching lid or plate.
5. Cook on FULL POWER for 6 minutes, stirring 3 times.
6. Stir in the vegetables and seasoning. Re-cover and cook on REHEAT for 1 minute.

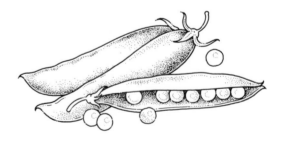

Devilled Black-eyed Bean Casserole

Serves 4

1½lb (675g) potatoes, peeled and chopped into 1in (2.5cm) pieces

3 tblsp water

2oz (50g) vegetable fat

3 tblsp milk

sea salt and freshly-milled black pepper to taste

12oz (350g) black-eyed beans, soaked overnight in water

boiling water

3oz (75g) onion, peeled and chopped

5oz (150g) carrots, peeled and diced

8oz (225g) blanched tomatoes, peeled and chopped

1 level tblsp tomato purée

1 level tblsp whole grain mustard

2 tblsp Worcestershire sauce

2 tblsp water

The mustard and Worcestershire sauce together give this dish a certain 'bite'. It is not essential to mash the beans, but the texture is much better if you do.

1. Place potatoes in a large glass basin with water. Cover with a plate then cook on FULL POWER for 12 minutes, stirring after 6 minutes.

2. Mash with 1oz (25g) vegetable fat, then beat in the milk and seasoning. Leave aside temporarily.

3. Place black-eyed beans in a 3½pt (2l) glass or pottery dish. Add sufficient boiling water to come ½in (1.25cm) over the top. Cover with cling film, then puncture twice with the tip of a knife.

4. Cook on FULL POWER for 15 minutes, keep covered and leave to stand for 10 minutes.

5. Place remaining vegetable fat in a small glass or pottery dish with the onion and carrots. Cover with a plate and cook on FULL POWER for 4 minutes until the carrots are just tender.

6. Drain off excess water from the beans and mash. Stir in cooked vegetables with remaining ingredients. Adjust seasoning and mix well.

7. Press mixture down lightly with a fork and cover with potato.

8. Cook on REHEAT for 5 minutes. (If liked the potato may be browned under a hot grill.)

Red Bean Curry

Serves 6

1lb (450g) red kidney beans, soaked overnight in water

1½pt (900ml) boiling water

1lb (450g) cauliflower, broken into small florets

1pt (600ml) boiling water

1lb (450g) tomatoes

¼pt (150ml) water

2oz (50g) creamed coconut

4oz (125g) onion, chopped

4oz (125g) green pepper, de-seeded, and sliced into 1½in (4cm) strips

2 green chillies, de-seeded and very finely chopped

3oz (75g) roasted peanuts

½ level tsp ground turmeric

½ level tsp ground cumin

1 level tsp ground coriander

1½ level tsp garam masala

2 level tsp sea salt

2 rounded tblsp fresh coriander leaves, chopped

A lovely, fragrant curry that can be made just as hot as you like with the addition of more green chillies.

1. Put the drained red beans into a 4pt (2.25l) glass or pottery mixing bowl with the 1½pt (900ml) boiling water. Cover with cling film and puncture twice with the tip of a knife. Cook on FULL POWER for 45 minutes. Remove from the oven and allow to stand for 15 minutes.

2. Put cauliflower florets into a 3pt (1.75l) glass or pottery bowl and pour over the 1pt (600ml) boiling water. Cover with cling film and puncture twice with the tip of a knife. Cook on FULL POWER for 6 minutes.

3. Strain the beans and cauliflower. Put them together into a 4pt (2.25l) glass or pottery bowl. Leave aside temporarily.

4. Put the tomatoes into a 2pt (1.2l) glass or pottery bowl and pour in the ¼pt (150ml) water. Cover with cling film and puncture twice with the tip of a knife. Cook on FULL POWER for 5 minutes. Remove from the oven, peel off skins then purée tomatoes in a food processor or blender. Tip into bowl. While tomato purée is still hot, stir in the creamed coconut. Continue stirring until it has melted completely.

5. Add the onion, pepper, chillies and peanuts to the bean and cauliflower mixture.

6. Blend the turmeric, cumin, coriander, garam masala and sea salt in a small jug or cup with a little of the purée tomato to form a curry paste.

7. Mix remaining tomato purée with beans and cauliflower etc, then stir in the curry paste. Mix well and add 1 tablespoon of the fresh coriander leaves. Cover with cling film and puncture twice with the tip of a knife. Cook on FULL POWER for 10 minutes.

8. Remove cling film and stir well. Return to the oven and cook uncovered on FULL POWER for a further 5 minutes.

9. Sprinkle with the remaining coriander leaves and serve with Indian Spice Rice (page 61).

Serves 4

4oz (125g) flageolet beans soaked in water overnight

boiling water

1oz (25g) vegetable fat

3oz (75g) onion, thinly sliced

2 level tsp paprika

3 large blanched and peeled tomatoes, chopped

½ level tsp chopped fresh thyme or good pinch of dried thyme

6oz (125g) medium hard garlic-flavoured tofu

sea salt and freshly-milled black pepper

Tofu with Flageolet Beans

This protein-packed side dish is very quick and easy to prepare.

1. Drain flageolet beans then place in a 3½pt (2l) glass or pottery dish. Add sufficient boiling water to come ½in (1.25cm) over the top of the beans. Cover with a matching lid or plate. Stand on a plate in case the water boils over.

2. Cook on FULL POWER for 25 minutes. Keep covered and leave to stand for 10 minutes.

3. Place vegetable fat, onion, and paprika in a small glass or pottery dish. Cover with a plate then cook on FULL POWER for 3 minutes.

4. Drain beans. Stir in onion mixture, tomatoes and thyme with a wooden spoon.

5. Cut tofu into 1in (2.5cm) pieces and stir into the vegetables with the seasoning. Cover with a plate and cook on REHEAT for 5 minutes. Accompany with boiled potatoes and a crisp green salad.

Lemony Chick Pea and Aubergine Casserole with Sesame Dumplings

Serves 4

8oz (225g) chick peas, soaked overnight in water

boiling water

1oz (25g) vegetable fat

4oz (125g) green pepper, seeds removed and thinly sliced

6oz (175g) onion, chopped

4oz (125g) aubergine, chopped into ¾in (2cm) pieces

juice of 1 lemon

1 level tblsp tahini

2 level tblsp chopped parsley

1 level tsp vegetable stock extract

¾pt (450ml) boiling water

sea salt and freshly-milled black pepper to taste

Dumplings

4oz (125g) self raising wholemeal flour

sea salt

2oz (50g) vegetable fat

cold water to mix

1 level tblsp sesame seeds

A cheerful all-rounder for family eating.

1. Drain chick peas then place in a 3½pt (2l) glass or pottery casserole. Add sufficient boiling water to come ½in (1.25cm) over the top. Cover with a matching lid then stand on a plate in case the water boils over.

2. Cook on FULL POWER for 25 minutes then leave to stand for 10 minutes.

3. Place vegetable fat in a 3½pt (2l) glass or pottery mixing bowl with pepper, onion and aubergine. Cover with a plate then cook on FULL POWER for 4 minutes, stirring half way through cooking.

4. Stir in lemon juice, tahini and parsley. Re-cover then cook on FULL POWER for a further 3 minutes.

5. Drain chick peas then stir in vegetable mixture.

6. Combine vegetable stock extract with boiling water. Pour into casserole with seasoning. Cover and leave to one side.

7. To make dumplings, stir flour and salt into a mixing bowl, rub in fat, then stir in enough water to form a firm dough. Shape into 8 balls.

8. Roll each ball in sesame seeds and press lightly to ensure that the seeds stick.

9. Place dumplings on top of vegetables. Cook, uncovered, on FULL POWER for 4 minutes. Leave to stand for 5 minutes before serving.

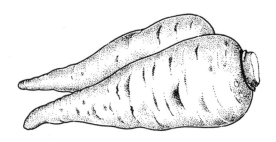

Serves 4

Filling

8oz (225g) split red lentils

1lb (450g) parsnips, peeled and chopped into 1in (2.5cm) pieces

boiling water

1oz (25g) vegetable fat

1 medium leek, washed and thinly sliced

sea salt and freshly-milled black pepper to taste

Crumble

3oz (75g) wholewheat breadcrumbs

1oz (25g) tamari roasted sunflower seeds

2oz (50g) Cheddar cheese, grated

Parsnip and Lentil Crumble

A crumble with a lovely nutty texture that's an economical dish and quick to prepare. If you cannot buy the tamari roasted sunflower seeds, substitute plain sunflower seeds. It is excellent served with a lemon and parsley sauce.

1. Place lentils and parsnips into a 3½pt (2l) glass bowl. Add sufficient boiling water to come ½in (1.25cm) over the top.
2. Cover with cling film then puncture twice with the tip of a knife. Stand on a plate in case the water boils over.
3. Cook on FULL POWER for 10 minutes. Keep covered and leave to stand for a further 10 minutes.
4. Place vegetable fat and leek in a small glass or pottery dish. Cover with a plate then cook on FULL POWER for 3 minutes. Stir leeks into lentil mixture with seasoning. Press mixture down lightly with a fork.
5. Mix breadcrumbs, sunflower seeds and cheese together. Sprinkle over the lentils.
6. Cook on REHEAT for 3 minutes. (If liked the crumble may be browned under a hot grill.)

29

Creamy Kidney Bean Wholewheat Pancakes

Serves 4

4oz (125g) red kidney beans, soaked overnight in water

boiling water

4oz (125g) wholewheat flour

1 grade 4 egg, beaten

½pt (300ml) skimmed milk

4 tblsp rape seed oil

5.29oz (150g) carton thick set yogurt

4oz (125g) goats' cheese (e.g. Chevre blanc)

1 level tblsp chopped fresh basil

sea salt and freshly-milled black pepper to taste

1oz (25g) vegetable fat

To garnish

chopped parsley

4 lemon wedges

Sophisticated and well-flavoured pancakes which should be accompanied by a crisp mixed salad.

1. Drain kidney beans, then place in a 2pt (1.25l) glass or pottery dish. Add sufficient boiling water to come ¾in (2cm) over the top. Cover with cling film, puncture twice with the tip of a knife. Stand on a plate in case the water boils over.

2. Cook on FULL POWER for 35 minutes. Check water level after 20 minutes and top up if necessary. Keep covered and leave to stand for 15 minutes.

3. Place wholewheat flour in a mixing bowl. Gradually beat in the egg and milk to make a smooth batter. On a CONVENTIONAL HOB, use batter to make 8 pancakes in the usual way, frying each in a little rape seed oil.

4. Drain beans. Finely chop in a blender or food processor. Add yogurt, goats' cheese, basil and seasoning. Blend for a further 30 seconds.

5. Divide the mixture between the pancakes and roll up. Place on a glass or pottery serving platter. Dot with vegetable fat, cover with cling film, and puncture twice with the tip of a knife.

6. Cook on ROAST for 6-8 minutes. Sprinkle with parsley and garnish with lemon wedges.

Tip
For speed, use canned kidney beans, adding them to the recipe at Point 4 above.

30

Green Pea Rissoles

Serves 4-6

8oz (225g) whole green peas, covered with boiling water and left to soak for 2 hours

boiling water

½oz (15g) vegetable fat

1 clove garlic, crushed

1 level tblsp chopped fresh chives

2 grade 4 eggs, beaten

3 tblsp milk

sea salt and freshly-milled black pepper to taste

1oz (25g) wholemeal flour

These rissoles can be prepared early in the day and cooked immediately before serving later on. Jacket potatoes are an appropriate accompaniment.

1. Drain peas, then place in a 3½pt (2l) glass or pottery dish. Add sufficient boiling water to come ½in (1.25cm) over the top. Cover with cling film and puncture twice with the tip of a knife. Stand on a plate in case water boils over.

2. Cook on FULL POWER for 30 minutes. Check water level after 20 minutes and top up if necessary. Keep covered and leave to stand for 10 minutes.

3. Place vegetable fat in a small glass or pottery dish with garlic and chives. Cover with a plate, then cook on FULL POWER for 2 minutes.

4. Drain peas then place in a blender or food processor with garlic, chives, eggs, milk and seasoning. Blend until smooth. Leave until cold.

5. Divide the mixture into 12 pieces. Shape into 3in (7.5cm) finger rolls on a lightly floured board.

6. Cook on FULL POWER in a pre-heated browning dish for 1½ minutes on each side. Remove from the oven and cover with aluminium foil to keep warm if required; otherwise serve straight away.

7. Accompany with a hot Balkan Tomato Sauce (page 118).

Red Kidney Bean Dip, à la Guacamole

Serves 4

6oz (175g) red kidney beans, soaked overnight in water

1pt (600ml) boiling water

2 ripe avocados

juice of 1 lemon

1 green chilli, de-seeded and very finely chopped

½ level tsp ground coriander

1 clove garlic, crushed

2 tblsp soya oil

4oz (125g) blanched tomatoes, skinned and chopped

½ level tsp chilli powder

sea salt and freshly-milled black pepper

A hot and spicy dip which is excellent served with sticks cut from fresh vegetables, toast or taco-type crisps. If you like it really hot, add more green chillies.

1. Put the drained soaked beans and the boiling water into a 3pt (1.75l) glass or pottery bowl. Cover with cling film and puncture twice with the tip of a knife. Cook on FULL POWER for 45 minutes. Allow to stand for 15 minutes. Drain.
2. Peel, stone and mash the avocados in a 2pt (1.2l) bowl. Add the lemon juice, chilli, coriander, garlic, oil, tomatoes, chilli powder and salt and pepper to taste.
3. Blend beans smoothly in a food processor or blender. Add to the avocado mixture and mix well.
4. Cover, chill well and serve.

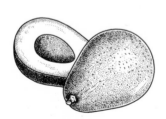

Mushroom Soup (p 13)
(Photo: Mushroom Growers' Association)

Lentil and Apple Loaf

The loaf is delicious served piping hot with a cider sauce, fried new potatoes and broccoli. It also makes ideal picnic fare if served cold with a mixed salad, or as a filling for sandwiches.

Serves 4-6

6oz (175g) split red lentils

2oz (50g) dried apple rings, chopped

boiling water

1oz (25g) vegetable fat

4oz (125g) onion, peeled and finely chopped

1 clove garlic, peeled and crushed

3oz (75g) carrot, peeled and grated

1oz (25g) hazelnuts, finely chopped

2 level tsp chopped fresh thyme or ½ level tsp dried thyme

1 tblsp chopped fresh parsley

1 grade 3 egg, beaten

sea salt and freshly-milled black pepper, to taste

1. Place lentils and apple in a 2pt (1.25l) glass or pottery dish. Add sufficient boiling water to come ½in (1.25cm) over the top. Cover with cling film, puncture twice with the tip of a knife. Stand on a plate in case the water boils over.

2. Cook on FULL POWER for 5 minutes. Keep covered and leave to stand for 10 minutes.

3. Place vegetable fat, onion and garlic in a small glass or pottery dish. Cover with a plate, then cook on FULL POWER for 3 minutes.

4. Drain off any excess water from the lentils then stir in onion mixture with the remaining ingredients. Mix well.

5. Turn into a lightly greased 1¼pt (750ml) glass loaf dish. Cover with cling film, then puncture twice with the tip of a knife.

6. Cook on FULL POWER for 5 minutes, then ROAST for 8 minutes. Turn loaf out and serve.

Above: Chilled Lettuce and Cucumber Soup (p 15)
(Photo: Vecon)
Below: Red Lentil and Apple Pate (p 20)
(Photo: Apple and Pear Development Council)

Serves 4-6

8oz (225g) black beans, soaked overnight in water

boiling water

1oz (25g) vegetable fat

8oz (225g) green cabbage, finely shredded

6oz (175g) carrots, thinly sliced

6oz (175g) onion, chopped

4oz (125g) open cup mushrooms, wiped clean and sliced

2 level tsp cornflour

3 tblsp organic cider vinegar

1 level tsp vegetable stock extract

¾ pt (450ml) boiling water or half stock and half wine

sea salt and freshly-milled black pepper to taste

Topping

12 × 1in (2.5cm) thick slices wholemeal french stick

4oz (125g) vegetable fat

2oz (50g) Cheddar cheese, grated

Crusty Topped Black Bean Casserole

A tasty casserole with a crusty topping.

1. Drain black beans, then place in a 3½pt (2l) glass or pottery casserole. Add sufficient boiling water to come ½in (1.25cm) over the top. Cover with matching lid. Stand on a plate in case the water boils over.

2. Cook on FULL POWER for 20 minutes. Keep covered and leave to stand for 10 minutes.

3. Place vegetable fat, cabbage, carrots and onion in a large glass or pottery dish. Cover with a plate, then cook on FULL POWER for 6 minutes.

4. Stir in mushrooms with a wooden spoon. Re-cover. Cook on FULL POWER for a further 3 minutes.

5. Drain black beans and mix in cooked vegetables.

6. Blend cornflour with the vinegar. Mix vegetable stock extract with the boiling water. Stir both ingredients into the casserole with the seasoning.

7. Spread the bread slices with vegetable fat and arrange on top of casserole, fat side up. Sprinkle with cheese.

8. Cook, uncovered, on FULL POWER for 4 minutes. Leave to stand for a further 5 minutes before serving.

Gnocchi

Serves 4

1pt (600ml) skimmed milk

1 small onion, coarsely chopped

1 bay leaf

6 level tblsp semolina

1oz (25g) vegetable fat

2oz (50g) mature Cheddar cheese, grated

1 level tblsp Parmesan cheese

2 grade 3 eggs, beaten

sea salt and freshly-milled black pepper to taste

½ level tsp poppy seeds

A lovely, classic Italian dish that should be served with heated-up canned tomatoes or creamed spinach.

1. Place milk, onion and bay leaf in a large glass or pottery dish. Cover with cling film, then puncture twice with the tip of a knife.
2. Cook on FULL POWER for 8 minutes. Remove from microwave and leave to stand for 3 minutes.
3. Strain milk and discard flavourings. Return to dish.
4. Stir semolina into milk, leave uncovered and return to microwave. Cook on FULL POWER for 6 minutes, stirring 3 times.
5. Add vegetable fat, cheeses and 1 beaten egg. Mix well and season to taste.
6. Spread mixture into an oiled 10in (25cm) shallow glass or pottery dish and leave until cold.
7. Using a 2½in (6cm) round fluted cutter, cut gnocchi into 10 to 11 rounds. Arrange trimmings on a 10in (25cm) greased plate, then top with Gnocchi rounds.
8. Brush heavily with beaten egg.
9. Sprinkle with poppy seeds and cook on REHEAT for 2 minutes.

Tip
Serve as an alternative to a potato topping by arranging rounds of Gnocchi over the surface of your chosen dish. Sprinkle with cheese and flash under a hot grill or reheat in the microwave.

Cannellini with French Beans and Salad

Serves 4

1lb (450g) potatoes, washed and scrubbed

1 grade 3 egg

sea salt and freshly-milled black pepper to taste

1 tblsp rape seed oil

4oz (125g) onion, peeled and finely chopped

4oz (125g) carrots, peeled and sliced

1 clove garlic, crushed

1 level tblsp wheatmeal flour

½ level tsp vegetable stock extract

½pt (300ml) boiling water

1 level tblsp tomato purée

½ level tsp fresh mixed herbs

3oz (75g) french beans, topped and tailed

14½oz (400g) can cannellini beans

An attractive side dish which would complement any meal.

1. Cut each medium potato into 8 pieces and larger ones into 16. Place in a 3½pt (2l) glass or pottery dish with 4 tablespoons of water. Cover with cling film then puncture twice with the tip of a knife.

2. Cook on FULL POWER for 10 minutes. Leave to stand for 5 minutes.

3. Purée the potato in a blender or food processor with the egg and seasoning. Using a forcing bag fitted with a large star nozzle, pipe potato around the edge of a shallow 10in (25cm) greased glass or pottery dish or casserole lid.

4. Place oil in a small glass or pottery dish with onion, carrots and garlic. Cook on FULL POWER for 2 minutes. Stir in flour.

5. Dissolve vegetable stock extract in ½pt (300ml) boiling water. Stir gradually into carrot mixture.

6. Cook on FULL POWER for 2 minutes then stir in the tomato purée, mixed herbs, french beans and cannellini beans.

7. Turn mixture into the centre of the potato and cook on REHEAT for 5 minutes, or until thoroughly heated through. Serve hot.

NUTS

All the nut specialities one can possibly think of
have been included in this section but the Mixed
Nut Pâté, Walnut and Potato Pie, White Nut and
Horseradish Ring, Chestnut and Celery Cake . . .
these are all something special and cook to
perfection in the microwave. One useful tip:
increase colour, keep all skins on nuts unless
otherwise stated in the recipe.

Mixed Nut Rolls with Cheese Pastry

Serves 4

8oz (225g) potatoes, cut into ¾in (2cm) dice

2 tblsp water

1oz (25g) vegetable fat

2oz (50g) onion, finely chopped

4oz (125g) mixed nuts, e.g. cashews, walnuts or brazil nuts, all very finely chopped

1 tsp sweet soy sauce

pinch of hot chilli powder

sea salt and freshly-milled black pepper to taste

Cheese Pastry

2oz (50g) vegetable fat

4oz (125g) wholewheat flour

2oz (50g) Double Gloucester and Chive cheese, finely-grated

cold water to mix

Extra crisp and crunchy when cold and perfect with pickles and salad for a summer lunch. Or try hot as a main course with vegetables.

1. Place potatoes in a glass or pottery mixing bowl with water. Cover with cling film, puncture twice with the tip of a knife.
2. Cook on FULL POWER for 5 minutes, stirring half way through cooking. Keep covered and leave to stand for 5 minutes.
3. Place vegetable fat and onion in a small bowl. Cover and cook on FULL POWER for 2 minutes.
4. Drain potatoes and mash until smooth. Beat in the cooked onion mixture, mixed nuts, sweet soy sauce, chilli powder and seasoning. Cool.
5. Shape into 8 finger rolls, each 3½in (9cm) long.
6. To make pastry, rub fat into flour then stir in cheese and enough cold water to form a fairly stiff dough.
7. Roll out to a rectangle and trim to 6in × 7in (15cm × 18cm). Mark the longer edge into 8, and cut into strips. Wind strips around the nut rolls in a spiral.
8. Place on a glass or pottery plate lined with a double thickness of kitchen paper. Place another double layer on top.
9. Cook on FULL POWER for 4 minutes. Remove top layers of paper and cook on FULL POWER for 2 minutes.
10. Quickly cover with aluminium foil and leave to stand for 5 minutes.
11. Serve hot with vegetables or cold with salad.

Tip

Double Gloucester cheese may be used without the addition of chives.

Walnut and Potato Pie

Serves 4

*1lb (450g) potatoes, cut into
¾in (2cm) dice*

6oz (175g) carrots, sliced

3 tblsp water

1oz (25g) vegetable fat

3oz (75g) onion, chopped

1 to 2 tsp paprika

1oz (25g) wholewheat flour

¾pt (450ml) skimmed milk

6oz (175g) walnuts, chopped

*sea salt and freshly-milled
black pepper to taste*

*2oz (50g) bulgar wheat,
soaked in cold water for 10
minutes, then drained*

*3oz (75g) Cheddar cheese,
grated*

To garnish

chopped parsley

A hearty main meal, well-endowed with protein.

1. Put potatoes, carrots and water into a 3pt (1.75l) glass or pottery casserole. Cover with a matching lid.
2. Cook on FULL POWER for 8 minutes, stirring half way through cooking. Keep covered and leave to stand for 5 minutes.
3. Put vegetable fat, onion and paprika into a 2pt (1.2l) glass or pottery dish. Cover with cling film and puncture twice with the tip of a knife.
4. Cook on FULL POWER for 3 minutes. Sprinkle on the flour and mix well. Gradually stir in the milk.
5. Cook, uncovered, on FULL POWER for 5 minutes, stirring half way through cooking. Stir in the walnuts and seasoning. Pour on to potatoes and carrots. Mix well.
6. Mix bulgar wheat and cheese together then sprinkle over potato mixture.
7. Cook, uncovered, on ROAST for 4 minutes. Sprinkle with parsley.
8. Serve with grilled tomato halves sprinkled with chopped basil and marjoram and a green vegetable.

Lemony Wheat with Brazils and Peanuts

Serves 4

8oz (225g) wholewheat grain, covered with boiling water and left to soak for 2 hours

boiling water

1oz (25g) vegetable fat

2 medium leeks, washed and thinly sliced

juice of 1 large lemon

3oz (75g) brazil nuts, coarsely chopped

3oz (75g) large salted peanuts

sea salt and freshly-milled black pepper

pinch of paprika

Another main course that tastes equally good hot or cold. Try serving it with green beans and a crisp salad.

1. Drain wholewheat then put in a 2pt (1.2l) glass or pottery casserole. Add sufficient boiling water to come ½in (1.25cm) over the top. Cover with a matching lid or plate. Stand on a plate in case water boils over.
2. Cook on FULL POWER for 10 minutes. Keep covered and leave to stand for 6 minutes. Drain.
3. Place vegetable fat in the casserole with leeks.
4. Cover then cook on FULL POWER for 3 minutes, stirring half way through cooking.
5. Stir in wholewheat, lemon juice and nuts.
6. Cover and cook on REHEAT for 4 minutes.
7. Stir in seasonings and serve.

Hazelnut, Garlic and Rosemary Loaf

Serves 4

1¼oz (40g) vegetable fat

8oz (225g) onions, chopped

2 garlic cloves, crushed

5oz (150g) wholemeal bread

1 sprig rosemary

A fine-flavoured loaf which goes well with parsley sauce or a rich and garlicky mayonnaise. Even mild mustard alone complements all the flavours of the dish.

2 sprigs parsley

8oz (225g) hazelnuts

2 grade 4 eggs, beaten

¼pt (150ml) water

sea salt and freshly-milled black pepper to taste

1. Put vegetable fat into a glass or pottery mixing bowl with the onions and garlic. Cover with cling film and puncture twice with the tip of a knife.
2. Cook on FULL POWER for 4 minutes, lifting film and stirring half way through.
3. Put bread and herbs into a food processor or blender and blend for 30 seconds. Add hazelnuts and blend for a further 30 seconds.
4. Stir nut mixture into onion and mix well. Beat in eggs, water and seasoning.
5. Turn mixture into a 1¼pt (750ml) glass loaf dish, base-lined with greaseproof paper.
6. Cover with cling film and puncture twice with the tip of a knife. Cook on FULL POWER for 5 minutes, then ROAST for 5 minutes. Keep covered and leave to stand for 4 minutes.
7. Turn out, cut into slices and serve as suggested. Accompany with baby new potatoes.

White Nut and Horseradish Ring

Serves 4

1oz (25g) vegetable fat

6oz (175g) onion, very finely chopped

4oz (125g) cashew nuts, very finely chopped

3oz (75g) brazil nuts, very finely chopped

2oz (50g) blanched almonds, very finely chopped

4oz (125g) fresh white breadcrumbs

1 to 1½ level tblsp freshly grated horseradish or 2 to 3 level tblsp horseradish sauce

3 grade 4 eggs, beaten

sea salt and freshly-milled black pepper

A handsome-looking and fine-tasting nut ring for special occasions. It is especially good hot with gravy and mixed vegetables. Also cold with a thick and creamy mayonnaise and a large bowl of french-dressed green salad.

1. Place vegetable fat and onion in a small glass or pottery mixing bowl. Cover with cling film and puncture twice with the tip of a knife.
2. Cook on FULL POWER for 3 minutes.
3. Stir in the remaining ingredients and mix well.
4. Line a 9in (23cm) glass ring mould with cling film. Spread nut mixture evenly into the lined mould and cover with cling film. Puncture twice with the tip of a knife.
5. Cook on ROAST for 5 minutes. Keep covered and leave to stand for 4 minutes. Turn out on to a plate and remove cling film. Serve hot or cold.

White Nut Cutlets with Cheese and Herbs

Makes 4

4oz (125g) cashew nuts, very finely chopped

2oz (50g) hazelnuts, very finely chopped

2oz (50g) white breadcrumbs

3oz (75g) Caerphilly cheese, grated

1 level tsp chopped fresh thyme or large pinch of dried thyme

An extremely quick and easy dish.

1. Place all ingredients into a mixing bowl and stir well to combine.

1 level tblsp chopped parsley

1 grade 4 egg, beaten

3 tblsp skimmed milk

sea salt and freshly-milled black pepper

Serves 4

¼ level tsp vegetable stock extract

¼pt (150ml) boiling water

1 small cauliflower, divided into small florets

14oz (400g) can chopped peeled tomatoes

4oz (125g) onion, finely chopped

2 sprigs fresh mint, finely chopped

6oz (175g) courgettes, sliced

3 level tsp cornflour

3 tsp water

sea salt and freshly-milled black pepper to taste

4oz (125g) self raising wholemeal flour

2oz (50g) vegetable fat

2oz (50g) hazelnuts, very finely chopped

cold water to mix

2. Divide into 4 and shape into round cutlets.
3. Pre-heat browning dish according to the manufacturer's instructions.
4. Cook cutlets in the pre-heated browning dish for 1½ minutes each side on FULL POWER. Allow to stand for 1 minute before serving.

Mixed Vegetable Casserole with Nut Dumplings

An attractive and flavoursome way to serve cauliflower and courgettes, with accompanying light and fluffy nutty dumplings.

1. Mix vegetable stock extract and boiling water together. Stir until dissolved.
2. Place cauliflower, chopped tomatoes and juice, onion, mint and vegetable stock in a 2½pt (1.5l) round casserole. Cover with a matching lid.
3. Cook on FULL POWER for 5 minutes, stirring half way through cooking.
4. Stir in courgettes. Blend cornflour with water until smooth, then stir into casserole with seasoning.
5. Cover and cook on FULL POWER for 10 minutes, stirring twice.
6. Stir flour and a pinch of salt into a mixing bowl. Rub in fat. Stir in nuts and enough water to form a fairly stiff dough. Shape into 8 balls.
7. Place dumplings on top of vegetables. Cook, uncovered, on FULL POWER for 4 minutes. Leave to stand for 5 minutes before serving.

43

Mushroom and Nut Meat Pudding

Serves 4-6

5oz (150g) vegetable fat
4oz (125g) onion, chopped
4oz (125g) carrots, diced
6oz (175g) cup mushrooms, wiped clean and chopped
¼ level tsp vegetable stock extract
7fl oz (200ml) boiling water
3 level tblsp flour
sea salt and freshly-milled black pepper
2 level tblsp chopped parsley
8oz (225g) self raising wholemeal flour
cold water to mix
12 oz (350g) leftover nut loaf (page 40), cubed

Although this recipe takes a little longer than most dishes, the results are well worth the extra effort. The pudding can be served direct from the basin but it certainly looks more impressive if turned out.

1. Place 1oz (25g) of vegetable fat into a small glass or pottery mixing bowl with onion and carrots. Cover with cling film and puncture twice with the tip of a knife.
2. Cook on FULL POWER for 4 minutes, stirring half way through cooking.
3. Stir in mushrooms. Cover and cook on FULL POWER for 2 minutes.
4. Mix vegetable stock extract and boiling water together. Stir until dissolved.
5. Sprinkle flour on to cooked vegetables and stir well. Gradually stir in vegetable stock and seasoning.
6. Cook, uncovered, on FULL POWER for 3 minutes, stirring well after each minute. Leave on one side temporarily.
7. Stir a pinch of salt, pepper and parsley into wholemeal flour. Rub in remaining vegetable fat. Mix to fairly stiff dough with water.
8. Roll out into a large circle, approximately 12in (30cm) in diameter. Remove one quarter of the round and reserve for lid. Use remainder to line a well-greased 2pt (1.2l) glass or pottery pudding basin.
9. Layer nut loaf and mushroom sauce into pudding basin, moisten pastry edges.
10. Roll out reserved pastry into a round, approximately 6in (15cm) and use to cover filling, sealing edges well.

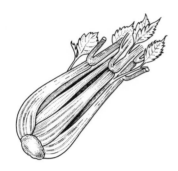

11. Loosely cover with cling film.
12. Cook on ROAST for 9 minutes. Keep covered and leave to stand for 6 minutes.
13. Carefully loosen sides of pudding with a knife and turn out on to a warm serving plate. Serve with Cranberry and Orange Sauce (page 124).

Chestnut and Celery Cake

Serves 6

4.41oz (125g) packet dried chestnuts, covered with boiling water and left to soak for 8 hours, or overnight

boiling water

1oz (25g) vegetable fat

6oz (175g) onion, very finely chopped

2 cloves garlic, crushed

3 large sticks celery, finely chopped

4oz (125g) wholemeal breadcrumbs

2 level tblsp chopped parsley

1 level tsp chopped fresh thyme or large pinch of dried thyme

5 sage leaves, finely chopped

6oz (175g) carrots, grated

¼pt (150ml) skimmed milk

1 grade 4 egg, beaten

sea salt and freshly-milled black pepper

A moist, savoury cake which can be served hot in wedges with a dish of shredded cabbage and crisply-fried diced potato. Alternatively, it can be served cold. A herb mayonnaise goes beautifully with the cold cake.

1. Drain chestnuts. Put into a large glass or pottery mixing bowl. Add sufficient boiling water to come ½in (1.25cm) over the top. Cover with cling film and puncture twice with the tip of a knife.
2. Cook on FULL POWER for 5 minutes. Keep covered and leave on one side temporarily.
3. Place vegetable fat in a glass or pottery mixing bowl with onion, garlic and celery. Cover.
4. Cook on FULL POWER for 4 minutes, stirring half way through cooking.
5. Stir in remaining ingredients. Drain chestnuts and finely chop. Stir into mixture and mix well.
6. Spread smoothly into a base-lined 3in (7.5cm) deep × 7in (18cm) round glass dish. Cover.
7. Cook on ROAST for 12 minutes. Keep covered and leave to stand for 6 minutes. Turn out and serve hot or cold.

Apple and Nut Stuffing Balls

Serves 4

4oz (125g) onion, grated

1lb (450g) Bramley apples, peeled, cored and thinly sliced

2oz (50g) unblanched almonds, very finely chopped

2 tblsp chopped parsley

4oz (125g) wholemeal breadcrumbs

1 grade 4 egg, beaten

sea salt and freshly-milled black pepper

a little wholemeal flour for shaping the balls

Together with a cucumber salad dressed with yogurt, these stuffing balls would be ideal served with any curry dish.

1. Put onion and apple into a 2pt (1.2l) glass or pottery bowl. Cover with cling film and puncture twice with the tip of a knife.
2. Cook on FULL POWER for 5 minutes. Break apple down into a purée with a fork.
3. Stir in the nuts, parsley, breadcrumbs, egg and seasoning.
4. Shape into 12 balls with floured hands.
5. Pre-heat the browning dish according to the manufacturer's instructions.
6. Cook nut balls on FULL POWER in the pre-heated browning dish for 3 minutes each side. Allow to stand for 1 minute before serving.

Mixed Nut Pâté

Serves 6

1oz (25g) vegetable fat

1 large stick celery, finely chopped

6oz (175g) onion, finely chopped

2 cloves garlic, crushed

4oz (125g) carrots, grated

3oz (75g) walnuts, finely chopped

3oz (75g) hazelnuts finely chopped

Serve this nutty pâté with wholemeal french bread, pickles, a mixed salad and a glass of wine. It makes a splendid summer lunch.

1. Place vegetable fat in a 1pt (600ml) glass or pottery dish with celery, onion and garlic. Cover with cling film, puncture twice with the tip of a knife.
2. Cook on FULL POWER for 3 minutes.
3. Put remaining ingredients into another 1pt (600ml) basin and mix well.

8oz (225g) chestnut *purée*

1 grade 4 egg, beaten

1 level tsp chopped fresh thyme

½ level tsp celery salt

¾ level tsp paprika

4. Stir in cooked vegetables. Turn into 1¼pt (750ml) glass loaf dish. Cover with cling film, puncture twice with the tip of a knife.

5. Cook on ROAST for 8 minutes. Keep covered and leave until cold. Turn out and serve in thick slices.

Serves 4

1oz (25g) vegetable fat

6oz (175g) onion, very finely chopped

3oz (75g) green pepper, very finely chopped

1 level tblsp wholemeal flour

¼pt (150ml) vegetable stock

2 level tsp mustard seed

4oz (125g) walnuts, very finely chopped

2oz (50g) unblanched almonds, very finely chopped

9oz (250g) malted wheat breadcrumbs

1 grade 4 egg, beaten

sea salt and freshly-milled black pepper

Walnut and Almond Nuggets

An economical dish that has an interesting soft texture. Serve with Spicy Root Vegetable Curry (page 102) and green beans.

1. Place vegetable fat, onion and green pepper into a glass or pottery mixing bowl. Cover with cling film and puncture twice with the tip of a knife.

2. Cook on FULL POWER for 3 minutes. Sprinkle flour over vegetables and stir well. Gradually mix in stock and mustard seed. Re-cover with lid or plate.

3. Cook on FULL POWER for 3 minutes, stirring well after each minute.

4. Stir in remaining ingredients and mix well.

5. Preheat browning dish according to manufacturer's instructions.

6. Drop 12 large spoons of mixture on to the pre-heated browning dish.

7. Cook on FULL POWER for 2½ minutes each side. Allow to stand for 2 minutes before serving.

47

Sweet 'n' Sour Tofu and Cashew Casserole

Serves 4

10½oz (297g) packet tofu, carefully drained

1oz (25g) vegetable fat

6oz (175g) onion, sliced lengthways into thin wedges

6oz (175g) carrots, sliced

6oz (175g) green pepper, seeds removed and cut into strips

6oz (175g) cup mushrooms, wiped clean and thickly sliced

2 tblsp soy sauce

1 tblsp dark syrup or black treacle

1 tblsp cider vinegar

¼pt (150ml) vegetable stock

2oz (50g) unsalted peanuts, very finely chopped

2oz (50g) raisins

1½oz (40g) dried banana, coarsely chopped

sea salt and freshly-milled black pepper

3oz (75g) cashew nuts, toasted

A nutritious dish packed full of protein and vitamins. Serve with brown rice sprinkled with chopped chives and parsley.

1. Place tofu on 2 pieces of absorbent kitchen paper and cover with another double layer of kitchen paper. Leave to one side temporarily.
2. Place vegetable fat, onion and carrots in a 3pt (1.75l) glass or pottery casserole. Cover with matching lid or plate.
3. Cook on FULL POWER for 3 minutes.
4. Stir in green pepper and mushrooms. Cover and cook on FULL POWER for 2 minutes.
5. Stir in all remaining ingredients, except tofu and toasted cashews. Cover and cook on FULL POWER for 3 minutes.
6. Carefully cut tofu into ¾in (2cm) pieces then stir into casserole. Cover.
7. Cook on REHEAT for 1½ minutes.
8. Sprinkle cashews on top. Serve hot.

Above: Curried Vegetable Risotto (p 50)
Below: Sweet N Sour Tofu and Cashew Casserole
(Photos: California Raisin Advisory Board)

_RICE AND PASTA

A wealth of 16 dishes based on rice and pasta have
been included and range from unusual Spaghetti
with Spicy Lentils to Cannelloni with Vegetable
Nut Stuffing. Rice and pasta in general take the
same time in the microwave as when cooked
conventionally, but there is minimal mess and no
sticky pans to clean up afterwards. When mixed
with boiling water, fresh pasta cooks in just 1
minute, wholemeal dried pasta is 'al dente' in 3,
and slow-cooking brown rice is ready in 25
minutes plus 10 minutes standing time compared
with the more customary 45 to 50 minutes when
boiled conventionally.

Above: Courgette, Baby Beet and Tomato Crumble
(p 89)
(Photo: Baxters of Speyside)
Below: Vegetarian Kebabs (p 109) with Barbecue Sauce
(p 120)
(Photo: British Alcan)

Curried Vegetable Risotto

Serves 4

2 tblsp rape seed oil

6oz (175g) onion, sliced

1in (2.5cm) root ginger,
peeled and finely chopped

4oz (125g) open cup
mushrooms, wiped and sliced

4oz (125g) red pepper, de-
seeded and sliced

4oz (125g) green pepper, de-
seeded and sliced

6oz (175g) cooking apples,
cored and chopped

6oz (175g) cauliflower,
separated into small florets

2 level tsp curry powder, mild
or hot as preferred

1 level tsp vegetable stock
extract

1pt (600ml) boiling water

6oz (175g) brown rice

1 rounded tblsp mango
chutney

2oz (50g) raisins

1oz (25g) vegetable fat

2oz (50g) unsalted peanuts

salt and freshly-milled pepper
to taste

A hearty, sweet-sour Risotto with a hint of curry. It is complete within itself but is also very much at home with a side salad of tomatoes sprinkled with lime juice.

1. Put oil, onion, ginger, mushrooms, red and green peppers, apple and cauliflower into a 3½pt (2l) glass or pottery dish. Cover with cling film, then puncture twice with the tip of a knife.

2. Cook on FULL POWER for 3 minutes.

3. Add curry powder and stir. Re-cover. Cook for a further 2 minutes on FULL POWER.

4. Dissolve vegetable stock extract in the boiling water, then add to the vegetable mixture with the rice, chutney and raisins. Re-cover with a lid or plate.

5. Return to the microwave and cook on FULL POWER for 25 minutes or until all the liquid has been absorbed by the rice. Stir 3 times during the cooking period.

6. Leave to stand for 10 minutes.

7. Meanwhile, put vegetable fat into a small glass bowl and add the peanuts. Cook on FULL POWER for 3 minutes. Drain peanuts on absorbent kitchen paper then stir peanuts into the risotto with seasoning.

Cheese and Rice Salad

Serves 4

4oz (125g) long grain brown rice
1pt (600ml) boiling water
4oz (125g) Cheddar cheese, cut into small dice
3in (7.5cm) cucumber, cut into small dice
1 stick celery, thinly sliced
2oz (50g) seedless raisins
1oz (25g) pumpkin seeds
2 tblsp walnut oil
1 tblsp lemon juice
½ tsp Worcestershire sauce
sea salt and freshly-milled black pepper to taste

An interesting salad, made slightly different by the addition of pumpkin seeds. As a change from Cheddar, use any other firm cheese such as Cheshire or Leicester.

1. Place rice in a 3½pt (2l) glass or pottery dish with 1pt (600ml) of boiling water. Cover with cling film then puncture twice with the tip of a knife.
2. Cook on FULL POWER for 25 minutes or until tender and all the water has been absorbed. Leave to cool.
3. Add the cheese, cucumber, celery, raisins and pumpkin seeds. Mix well.
4. Whisk together oil, lemon juice, Worcestershire sauce, and seasoning. Stir into the rice mixture.
5. Turn into a serving dish, cover and refrigerate until lightly-chilled.

Serves 4

4oz (125g) wholemeal
lasagne

½ tsp oil

½ level tsp vegetable stock
extract

1¼pt (750ml) boiling water

4oz (125g) split red lentils

2oz (50g) French Puy lentils
or split red lentils again

4oz (125g) onion, thinly
sliced

2 sticks celery, chopped

6 fresh sage leaves, finely
chopped

¾pt (450ml) boiling water

1½oz (40g) vegetable fat

1½oz (40g) wholemeal flour

¾pt (450ml) skimmed milk

3oz (75g) strong Cheddar
cheese, grated

sea salt and freshly-milled
black pepper to taste

4oz (125g) tomatoes, sliced

½oz (15g) grated Parmesan
cheese

Mixed Lentil Lasagne

A tasty and sustaining lasagne, made for a robust mixed salad which has been snappily dressed with Sauce Vinaigrette.

1. Place lasagne in a large, oblong glass casserole with oil and sufficient boiling water for it to float. Cover with cling film and puncture twice with the tip of a knife.

2. Cook on FULL POWER for 7 minutes. Keep covered and leave to stand for 15 minutes. Drain and rinse.

3. Mix vegetable stock extract and boiling water together. Stir until dissolved.

4. Place lentils, onion, celery, sage and vegetable stock into a glass or pottery mixing bowl. Cover with cling film. Puncture twice with the tip of a knife.

5. Cook on FULL POWER for 10 minutes, lifting film and stirring half way through cooking. Keep covered and leave on one side temporarily.

6. Melt vegetable fat in a glass measuring jug on FULL POWER for 30 seconds.

7. Sprinkle flour on to fat and stir well. Gradually stir in milk.

8. Cook on FULL POWER for 5 minutes, stirring well after each minute.

9. Stir in two-thirds of the Cheddar cheese and seasoning.

10. Arrange alternate layers of lentils, lasagne and cheese sauce in a 3pt (1.75l) glass oblong casserole, finishing with a layer of cheese sauce.

52

11. Sprinkle remaining Cheddar cheese over the top. Add slices of tomato then shower with Parmesan cheese.

12. Cover with cling film and cook on ROAST for 5 minutes. (If liked, brown under a pre-heated grill.)

Serves 4

8oz (225g) tagliatelli verdi
½ tsp oil
1½pt (900ml) boiling water
1½oz (40g) vegetable fat
3oz (75g) onion, thinly sliced
6oz (175g) green pepper, de-seeded and finely chopped
3 level tblsp scissor-snipped chives
5oz (150g) soft cream cheese
juice of 1 lemon
¼pt (150ml) single cream
sea salt and freshly-milled black pepper to taste
6oz (175g) walnuts, chopped

Tagliatelli with Creamy Walnut and Cheese Sauce

An elegant main course with a subtle flavour and texture. It can be prepared quickly and easily.

1. Put tagliatelli, oil and water into a 3pt (1.75l) glass or pottery casserole.

2. Cook, uncovered, on FULL POWER for 8 minutes, stirring half way through cooking. Cover then stand aside for 5 minutes. Drain then return to casserole.

3. Put vegetable fat, onion, pepper and chives into a large mixing bowl. Cover with cling film and puncture twice with the tip of a knife.

4. Cook on FULL POWER for 4 minutes.

5. Stir in remaining ingredients, cover and cook on ROAST for 1 minute.

6. Turn sauce on to tagliatelle and gently fold in. Cover and cook on ROAST for 3 minutes.

7. Serve with a colourful crisp salad topped with raw sliced mushrooms and pieces of peeled orange.

Tomato and Cashew Nut Savoury Rice

Serves 4 (as a side dish)

6oz (175g) natural brown rice

6oz (175g) tomatoes, peeled and chopped

2oz (50g) cashew nuts, chopped

2 level tblsp chopped parsley

grated rind of 1 lemon

1½ level tsp vegetable stock extract

1pt (600ml) boiling water

sea salt and freshly-milled black pepper to taste

The cashew nuts in this easy side dish enhance the natural nutty texture of the brown rice.

1. Place all the ingredients into a 3pt (1.75l) glass or pottery casserole. Cover with a matching lid.
2. Cook on FULL POWER for 35 minutes, stirring 3 times during cooking.
3. Keep covered and leave to stand for 10 minutes.
4. Serve as an accompaniment to main course dishes.

Cannelloni with Vegetable Nut Stuffing

Serves 4

8 sheets wholemeal lasagne

boiling water

8oz (225g) lightly cooked mixed vegetables: aubergine, beans onion, courgettes etc.

sea salt and freshly-milled black pepper to taste

1oz (25g) pumpkin seeds

1oz (25g) chopped mixed nuts

1 grade 3 egg

Balkan Tomato Sauce (page 118)

An attractive dish fit for any dinner party.

1. Place lasagne in a 3½pt (2l) large bowl and add sufficient boiling water to come ½in (1.25cm) over the top of the lasagne. Cover dish with cling film, then puncture twice with the tip of a knife.
2. Cook on FULL POWER for 3 minutes. Drain and lay sheets of lasagne on a chopping board or work surface.

3. Place mixed vegetables in a blender or food processor with seasoning. Blend for a few seconds until coarsely chopped.

4. Add pumpkin seeds, nuts and egg to vegetables and blend to incorporate.

5. Divide mixture between cooked lasagne and roll up. Place on a 10in (25cm) glass or pottery dish.

6. Coat with Tomato Sauce (page 118). Cover with lid. Place in microwave and cook on REHEAT for 5 minutes. Serve Hot.

Serves 4

3oz (75g) flageolet beans, soaked overnight

boiling water

½oz (15g) vegetable fat

2 cloves garlic, crushed

14oz (400g) can peeled tomatoes, chopped

4oz (125g) wholewheat macaroni

8oz (225g) courgettes, sliced

2 tsp English made mustard

½pt (300ml) boiling water

sea salt and freshly-milled black pepper

Macaroni and Flageolet Supper

An ideal family supper dish, best eaten with warm crusty herb bread to mop up the juices.

1. Drain beans, place them in a 2pt (1.2l) glass or pottery casserole. Add sufficient boiling water to come ½in (1.25cm) over the top. Cover with a matching lid or plate. Stand on a plate in case water boils over.

2. Cook on FULL POWER for 25 minutes. Keep covered and leave to stand for 10 minutes.

3. Place vegetable fat and garlic in a 3pt (1.75l) glass or pottery casserole. Cover with a matching lid or plate. Cook on FULL POWER for 1 minute.

4. Stir in remaining ingredients, plus the drained flageolet beans.

5. Cover and cook on FULL POWER for 15 minutes, stirring twice during cooking. Keep covered and leave to stand for 10 minutes.

Spaghetti with Spicy Lentils

Serves 4

1oz (25g) vegetable fat

6oz (175g) onion, chopped

3 sticks celery, chopped

8oz (225g) tomatoes, peeled and chopped

1 level tblsp tomato purée

1 level tsp ground coriander

½ level tsp ground cumin

½ level tsp ground ginger

4oz (125g) brown lentils, covered with boiling water and left to soak for 1 hour

boiling water

8oz (225g) wholewheat spaghetti

½ tsp oil

1½pt (900ml) boiling water

12 black olives, stones removed and coarsely chopped

1 level tblsp cornflour

½pt (300ml) strong cider

sea salt and freshly-milled black pepper to taste

The vegetarian answer to Spaghetti Bolognaise.

1. Put vegetable fat, onion, celery, tomatoes, tomato purée and spices into a glass or pottery mixing bowl. Cover with cling film and puncture twice with the tip of a knife.

2. Cook on FULL POWER for 5 minutes, lifting film and stirring half way through cooking. Keep covered and leave on one side temporarily.

3. Drain lentils then place in a 3pt (1.75l) glass or pottery casserole. Add sufficient boiling water to come ½in (1.25cm) over the top of the lentils. Cover with a matching lid or plate.

4. Cook on FULL POWER for 10 minutes. Keep covered and leave to stand for 10 minutes.

5. Place spaghetti, oil and water into a large glass or pottery mixing bowl.

6. Cook, uncovered, on FULL POWER for 7 minutes, stirring half way through cooking. Cover then leave to stand for 10 minutes.

7. Drain lentils then return to casserole. Stir in the cooked vegetables and olives.

8. Blend the cornflour with the cider until smooth. Stir into casserole with seasoning.

9. Cook, uncovered, on FULL POWER for 8 minutes, stirring 3 times during cooking.

10. Drain spaghetti then serve portions with the sauce spooned over the top. If liked, hand grated Parmesan cheese separately.

Cheesy Vegetable Lasagne

Serves 4

6oz (175g) lasagne

½tsp oil

1½pts (900ml) boiling water

1½oz (40g) vegetable fat

3oz (75g) onion, finely chopped

6oz (175g) courgettes, sliced

4oz (125g) green pepper

6oz (175g) aubergine, thinly sliced

1½oz (40g) wholewheat flour

¾pt (450ml) skimmed milk

1 tblsp whole grain mustard

sea salt and freshly-milled black pepper

4oz (125g) Cheddar cheese, grated

paprika pepper

A good filling supper dish.

1. Place lasagne in a large glass oblong casserole with oil and sufficient boiling water for it to float. Cover with cling film and puncture twice with the tip of a knife.
2. Cook on FULL POWER for 9 minutes. Keep covered and stand aside for 15 minutes. Drain and rinse.
3. Meanwhile put vegetable fat into a large glass or pottery mixing bowl with the vegetables. Cover with cling film and puncture twice with the tip of a knife. Cook on FULL POWER for 10 minutes, stirring half way through cooking.
4. Sprinkle flour on to vegetables and mix well. Gradually stir in the milk, mustard and seasoning.
5. Cook, uncovered, on FULL POWER for 4 minutes.
6. Arrange alternate layers of lasagne, vegetable sauce and cheese in a 3pt (1.75l) glass oblong casserole, finishing with a layer of cheese.
7. Sprinkle with paprika pepper.
8. Cover and cook on ROAST for 5 minutes.
9. Serve with warm crusty bread and a simple salad to complete the meal.

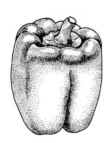

Sweet Fruit and Nut Risotto

Serves 3-4

2 tblsp rape seed oil

4oz (125g) brown rice

4oz (125g) onion, peeled and finely chopped

1 level tsp vegetable stock extract

1pt (600ml) boiling water

rind and juice of ½ lemon

small sprig fresh thyme

salt and freshly-milled pepper to taste

4oz (125g) white grapes, halved and pips removed

4oz (125g) black grapes, halved and pips removed

2oz (50g) blanched almonds

A smart Risotto, laced with almonds and grapes, which goes well with many vegetable main courses.

1. Place oil in a 3½pt (2l) glass or pottery dish. Add rice and onion then fry, uncovered, on FULL POWER for 3 minutes.

2. Dissolve vegetable stock extract in boiling water. Add lemon rind and juice. Pour into the bowl with the rice and onion. Add thyme and seasoning.

3. Cover with cling film then puncture twice with the tip of a knife. Cook on FULL POWER for 35 minutes. Remove lemon rind.

4. Stir in grapes and almonds. Leave to stand for 10 minutes.

5. Serve hot.

Serves 4

8oz (225g) wholemeal macaroni

boiling water

2 tblsp rape seed oil

6oz (175g) onion, sliced

½ level tsp chopped fresh basil or large pinch dried basil

8oz (225g) tomatoes, sliced

8oz (225g) Red Leicester cheese, grated

sea salt and freshly-milled black pepper to taste

2 level tablsp chopped parsley

Cheese, Tomato and Macaroni Casserole

A healthy and good-natured family main course, ideal for lunch or supper and mild enough to please fastidious children.

1. Put macaroni into a deep 3½pt (2l) glass or pottery bowl. Add sufficient boiling water to come ½in (1.25cm) over the top of the macaroni. Cover bowl with cling film then puncture twice with the tip of a knife.

2. Cook on FULL POWER for 3 minutes. Drain.

3. Put oil, onion and basil in a small glass or pottery dish. Cover with cling film then puncture twice with the tip of a knife. Cook on FULL POWER for 3 minutes.

4. Lightly oil a glass or pottery 2pt (1.2l) casserole dish and fill with alternate layers of macaroni, onion, tomatoes and cheese. Sprinkle seasoning between the layers and finish with grated cheese.

5. Cook, uncovered, on FULL POWER for 7 minutes.

6. Serve hot, sprinkled with parsley.

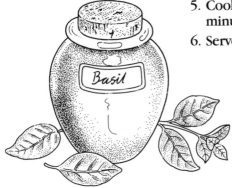

Rice and Beans

Serves 4

6oz (150g) red kidney beans, soaked overnight in water

4oz (125g) onion, peeled and finely chopped

1 clove garlic, finely chopped

1 level tsp chopped fresh thyme or ¼ level tsp dried thyme

1 — 2 fresh chillies, de-seeded and finely sliced

boiling water

8oz (225g) brown rice

1 level tsp sea salt

A hot, hot side dish to complement curries.

1. Drain soaked beans. Transfer to a 3½pt (2l) glass or pottery bowl. Mix in the onion, garlic, thyme and chillies. Add sufficient boiling water to come ½in (1.25cm) above the level of the beans.
2. Cover bowl with cling film then puncture twice with the tip of a knife. Cook on FULL POWER for 20 minutes.
3. Add rice and salt. Re-cover and cook for a further 25 minutes on FULL POWER until rice is tender and most of the water has been absorbed.

Noodles with Wensleydale Cheese, Tomatoes and Garlic

Serves 4

8oz (225g) wholewheat noodles

boiling water

3oz (75g) Wensleydale cheese, grated

2 tblsp olive oil

1lb (450g) blanched ripe tomatoes, peeled and quartered

3oz (75g) onion, peeled and chopped

2 cloves garlic, crushed

sea salt and freshly-milled black pepper

A very tempting cheesy side dish which would also be good as a supper dish for two people.

1. Place noodles in a 3½pt (2l) mixing bowl and cover with boiling water. Cook, uncovered, on FULL POWER for 4 minutes or until noodles are tender. Drain well and return noodles to bowl with the cheese and 1 tablespoon olive oil. Mix well. Cover and keep hot.

1 bayleaf

sprig of fresh thyme, parsley and basil

1 level tblsp wheatmeal flour

1oz (25g) Gruyère cheese

2 level tsp chopped parsley

2. Place remaining oil, tomatoes, onion, garlic, seasoning, herbs and flour into a 2pt (1.2l) glass or pottery dish. Cover with cling film then puncture twice with the tip of a knife.

3. Cook on FULL POWER for 8 minutes until soft and mushy. Pass through a sieve or vegetable mill. Alternatively, work to purée in blender goblet or food processor.

4. Arrange noodles in a large and shallow glass or pottery serving dish. Coat with tomato sauce and sprinkle with Gruyère cheese. Cook on REHEAT for 3 minutes or until heated through. Leave uncovered.

5. Garnish with chopped parsley and serve hot.

Serves 4

1oz (25g) vegetable fat

4oz (125g) onion, finely chopped

2 cloves garlic, crushed

½in (1.25cm) piece of fresh root ginger, peeled and grated

¼ level tsp hot chilli powder

1 level tsp garam masala

½ level tsp ground turmeric

sea salt and freshly-milled black pepper

4oz (125g) Basmati rice, rinsed 3 times then drained

½ level tsp vegetable stock extract

8fl oz (250ml) boiling water

Indian Spice Rice

A flavoursome rice dish to serve with main course curries.

1. Place vegetable fat, onion, garlic, ginger, spices and seasoning into a 3pt (1.75l) glass or pottery casserole. Cover with a matching lid.

2. Cook on FULL POWER for 3 minutes.

3. Stir in the rice. Blend vegetable stock extract with the boiling water and add to dish.

4. Cover and cook on FULL POWER for 7 minutes. Keep covered and leave to stand for 4 minutes. Stir round with a fork before serving.

Chinese-style Rice and Egg Scramble with Vegetables

Serves 4

4oz (125g) brown rice

1pt (600ml) boiling water

2 tblsp sunflower oil

1 small bunch spring onions, sliced into 1in (2.5cm) lengths

1 clove garlic, crushed

2 tblsp soy sauce

sea salt and freshly-milled black pepper

2 grade 3 eggs, beaten

2oz (50g) cooked peas

2oz (50g) cooked sweetcorn kernels

An appetising and fulfilling main course which should be served with bean sprouts and extra soy sauce. Also chilli sauce for heat.

1. Put rice into a 3½pt (2l) glass or pottery dish. Pour over the boiling water. Cover with cling film, then puncture twice with the tip of a knife.

2. Cook on FULL POWER for 25 minutes or until the rice is tender and the water has been absorbed. Leave to stand for 10 minutes.

3. Put oil, onion and garlic in a small glass or pottery bowl. Cook on FULL POWER for 3 minutes then add to the rice.

4. Mix soy sauce and seasoning with the beaten egg and stir into the hot rice so that the egg lightly scrambles. Mix well.

5. Stir in the peas and sweetcorn. Return to the microwave, cover with lid on plate and cook on FULL POWER for 6 minutes, stirring twice during cooking.

6. Serve piping hot.

Noodles with Caerphilly Cheese and Onions

Serves 4

6oz (175g) fresh wholemeal noodles

boiling water

2 tblsp safflower oil

12oz (350g) onion, finely chopped

12oz (350g) blanched tomatoes, peeled and sliced

2 cloves garlic, crushed

sea salt and freshly-milled black pepper

4 grade 3 eggs

3oz (75g) Caerphilly cheese

Fresh pasta, now readily available from supermarket chains and speciality food stores, takes well to microwave cooking and always turns out 'al dente'; pleasingly chewy but never too soft and bloated.

1. Put noodles in a 3½pt (2l) glass or pottery mixing bowl with enough boiling water to cover. Cover bowl with cling film, then puncture twice with the tip of a knife.

2. Cook on FULL POWER for one minute. Remove from oven, drain and rinse under cold water. Transfer to a 1pt (600ml) oval dish.

3. Put oil, onion, tomatoes, garlic and seasoning into a 2pt (1.2l) glass or pottery mixing bowl. Cover with lid or plate, then cook on FULL POWER for 6 minutes. Stir twice during cooking.

4. Spoon tomato mixture over noodles and, with the back of a large spoon, make four hollows in mixture for the eggs.

5. Crack eggs into hollows and puncture each yolk twice with a skewer. Sprinkle with cheese then cook, uncovered, on FULL POWER for 7 minutes. Serve immediately.

Rice with Mung Beans and Coconut Milk

Serves 4

4oz (125g) dried mung beans, soaked overnight in water

boiling water

4oz (125g) onion, peeled and finely chopped

1 tblsp rape seed oil

3 drops tabasco sauce

1oz (25g) creamed coconut, dissolved in 4 tblsp water (to make milk)

1 sprig fresh thyme

sea salt and freshly-milled black pepper

6oz (175g) brown rice

An exotic side dish with a harmonious blend of flavours.

1. Drain beans. Place in a 3½pt (2l) glass or pottery dish. Add sufficient boiling water to come ½in (1.25cm) over the top of the beans. Cover with cling film then puncture twice with the tip of a knife.
2. Cook on FULL POWER for 5 minutes. Drain and reserve cooking liquor. Return beans to basin.
3. Place oil in a small glass or pottery dish with onion and fry on FULL POWER for 3 minutes or until tender. Leave uncovered.
4. Add onion to beans with tabasco sauce, coconut milk, thyme, seasoning and rice. Pour over 16fl oz (475ml) of reserved cooking liquor (make up with water if insufficient).
5. Cover with cling film then puncture twice with the tip of a knife. Cook on FULL POWER for 25 minutes or until the rice is tender. Leave to stand for 10 minutes then serve.

EGGS AND CHEESE

The joy of cooking egg and cheese dishes in the microwave is that they all turn out superbly, with a delicacy of texture and flavour that is hard to achieve by conventional methods. Because eggs and cheese respond in this way to the microwave approach, there is a pick of 13 different dishes in this section and range from scrambled eggs to a stunning Curried Cheese Tart, an unusual Cheese and Beansprout Loaf, and a classic Cheese Fondue.

Eggs Florentine

Serves 4

8oz (225g) fresh spinach, washed and chopped

sea salt and freshly-milled black pepper to taste

4 grade 1 or grade 2 eggs

A quick and easy starter, and a very popular one.

1. Divide the chopped spinach equally between 4 glass or pottery ramekin dishes.
2. Arrange the dishes in the oven and cook, uncovered, on FULL POWER for 1½ minutes.
3. Remove from the oven and add the seasoning.
4. Carefully break 1 egg into each ramekin dish, over spinach. Prick the yolks twice with the tip of a knife.
5. Cook, uncovered, on ROAST for 4 minutes. Remove from the oven and rest for 1 minute. Serve hot with fingers of toast.

Scrambled Eggs

Serves 1

2 grade 3 eggs, at kitchen temperature

2 tblsp skimmed milk

sea salt and freshly-milled black pepper to taste

Variations

Before cooking add any of the following to the beaten eggs and milk:

pinch mixed dried herbs

or *1 1evel tsp chopped parsley*

or *1 level tsp chopped chives*

or *1 small blanched tomato, peeled and chopped*

Scrambled eggs made in the microwave are spectacular; deliciously creamy and a feast for any meal of the day.

1. Break the eggs into a 1pt (600ml) glass or pottery jug or bowl.
2. Add the milk and seasoning and beat well with a fork.
3. Cook, uncovered, on ROAST for 2½ minutes, stirring after every 30 seconds.
4. Rest for 1 minute then serve with toast.

Serves 4

1oz (25g) vegetable fat

6oz (175g) red pepper, seeds removed and finely chopped

4oz (125g) spring onions, finely chopped

8oz (225g) beansprouts, finely chopped

4oz (125g) wheatmeal breadcrumbs

4oz (125g) Cheddar cheese, grated

2 grade 4 eggs, beaten

sea salt and freshly-milled black pepper to taste

Cheese and Beansprout Loaf

A colourful and tasty savoury loaf which should be served with gravy and freshly-cooked, Chinese-style noodles.

1. Put vegetable fat in a 2pt (1.2l) glass or pottery mixing bowl with red pepper and spring onions. Cover with cling film and puncture twice with the tip of a knife.

2. Cook on FULL POWER for 3 minutes.

3. Uncover and stir in remaining ingredients. Mix well. Turn into a 1¼pt (750ml) glass loaf dish, greased and base-lined with paper. Press down lightly. Cover with cling film and puncture twice with the tip of a knife.

4. Cook on ROAST for 6 minutes. Keep covered and leave to stand for 5 minutes. Turn out on to a warm serving platter and cut into thick slices. Serve hot.

67

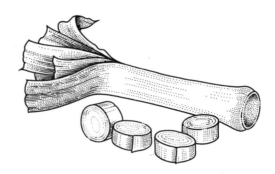

Egg and Leek Bake

Serves 4

1lb (450g) leeks, trimmed, half-slit and well-washed

6oz (175g) tomatoes, sliced

2 grade 3 eggs, at kitchen temperature

¼pt (150ml) single cream

salt and freshly-milled black pepper to taste

3oz (75g) Vegetarian Cheddar cheese

Choose four equal-sized and slender leeks for this chic supper dish.

1. Arrange leeks, side by side, in a glass or pottery rectangular dish 12in × 9in (30cm × 23cm). Place slices of tomato in between.
2. Cover with cling film and puncture twice with the tip of a knife. Remove plastic drive unit underneath turntable. Add dish of leeks and cook on FULL POWER for 3 minutes. Turn dish and cook on FULL POWER for a further 3 minutes.
3. Beat together the eggs, cream and seasoning. Pour over the leeks. Sprinkle with cheese.
4. Re-cover and puncture twice with the tip of a knife. Cook on FULL POWER for 3 minutes. Turn and cook on FULL POWER for a further 3 minutes.
5. Stand for 5 minutes then serve hot.

Egg and Lentil Curry

Serves 4

4oz (125g) split red lentils

6oz (175g) onion, chopped

2 cloves garlic, crushed

6oz (175g) carrots, finely chopped

2 large sticks celery, finely chopped

2 level tsp ground coriander

1 level tsp ground cumin

seeds of 6 opened-out cardamom pods

1in (2.5cm) cinnamon stick, lightly crushed

1 level tblsp tomato purée

½ level tsp vegetable stock extract

¾pt (450ml) hot water

sea salt and freshly-milled black pepper

4 grade 4 eggs

To garnish

chopped parsley

A simple-to-make and nutrition-packed curry which goes particularly well with Stuffed Mushrooms (page 97), garlic-flavoured poppadums and mango chutney.

1. Put all ingredients, except eggs, into a 3pt (1.75l) glass or pottery casserole. Cover with a matching lid or plate.
2. Cook on FULL POWER for 10 minutes, stirring 3 times during cooking. Keep covered and leave to stand for 7 minutes.
3. Hard boil eggs conventionally and shell. Cut each egg into quarters then place on top of curry.
4. Garnish with parsley.

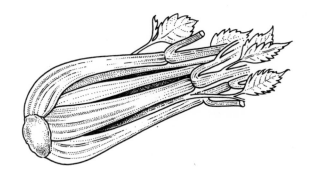

Creamy Eggs baked in Cabbage

Serves 4

2oz (50g) vegetable fat

1¼lb (500g) Savoy cabbage, finely-shredded

8oz (225g) onion, chopped

8oz (225g) potatoes, peeled and cut into matchsticks

¼pt (150ml) soured cream

2 level tblsp whole grain mustard

sea salt and freshly-milled black pepper

4 grade 4 eggs, at room temperature

Cabbage nests filled with eggs and cream — blissfully rich and reminiscent of Central European splendours. Serve with fresh green beans and puréed carrots tantalisingly flavoured with mace or nutmeg.

1. Put vegetable fat in a 2½pt (1.5l) glass or pottery mixing bowl. Cook, uncovered, on FULL POWER for 1 minute.

2. Stir in cabbage, onions and potatoes. Cover with cling film and puncture twice with the tip of a knife.

3. Cook on FULL POWER for 8 minutes, lifting film and stirring half way through cooking.

4. Stir in half the soured cream, mustard and seasoning. Mix well.

5. Turn into a round glass dish measuring 2in × 8in (5cm × 20cm).

6. Using the back of a wooden spoon, make 4 deep nests in the mixture then break an egg carefully into each. Puncture each yolk twice with a skewer. Coat with rest of cream.

7. Cook, uncovered, on REHEAT for 7 minutes. Leave to stand for 5 minutes.

Cheese and Carrot Pie with Wholemeal Pastry

Serves 4

4oz (125g) carrots, peeled and thinly sliced

2 tblsp water

2 tblsp safflower oil

3oz (75g) onion, finely chopped

2 large sticks celery, washed and sliced

4oz (125g) button mushrooms, sliced

2 level tblsp wheatmeal flour

½pt (300ml) skimmed milk

1 small sprig fresh thyme

sea salt and freshly-milled black pepper

4oz (125g) Cheddar cheese, cubed

Pastry

4oz (125g) wholemeal flour

2oz (50g) vegetable fat

2 tblsp cold water to mix

1 grade 3 egg, beaten

A mixed vegetable pie with tempting taste.

1. Put sliced carrot in a small glass or pottery bowl with 2 tablespoons water. Cover with cling film, then puncture twice with the tip of a knife.

2. Cook on FULL POWER for 5 minutes. Leave on one side temporarily.

3. Put oil, onion, celery and mushrooms into a small glass or pottery bowl. Cover as before and cook on FULL POWER for 3 minutes.

4. Stir flour into onion mixture and gradually add milk. Follow with the thyme, seasoning, cheese and cooked strained carrots.

5. Re-cover and cook on FULL POWER for 3 minutes to thicken mixture. Leave to cool, then transfer to a 10in (25cm) glass pizza dish or shallow plate.

6. To make pastry, sift flour into a bowl and rub in fat until the mixture resembles fine breadcrumbs. Fork-mix to a firm dough with water.

7. Roll out pastry and use to cover vegetable mixture. Press well down then glaze with beaten egg.

8. Cook, uncovered, on FULL POWER for 9 minutes.

Cheese and Potato Layer Pie

Serves 4

1½lb (675g) potatoes, washed and thinly sliced

5oz (150g) onion, sliced

6oz (175g) carrots, grated

8oz (225g) Red Leicester cheese, grated

1 level tblsp chopped parsley

1 level tsp chopped fresh mixed herbs or ¼ level tsp dried herbs

sea salt and freshly-milled black pepper to taste

¼pt (150ml) skimmed milk

An enjoyable casserole for winter eating which should be partnered with freshly-boiled and mashed swedes, a dish of peas and some pickled beetroot.

1. Fill a 2pt (1.2l) glass or pottery pie dish, well-greased, with alternate layers of potatoes, onion, carrots and cheese. Finish with a layer of potatoes and grated cheese.
2. Combine parsley, mixed herbs and seasoning with the milk. Pour gently down side of casserole.
3. Cover with cling film punctured twice with the tip of a knife.
4. Cook on FULL POWER for 25 minutes. Leave to stand for 10 minutes before serving.

Tip
Make sure the potatoes are very thinly sliced or the casserole will take longer to cook and may spoil.

Cheese Fondue

Serves 4

½ clove garlic

¼pt (150ml) dry white wine

1 tsp lemon juice

14oz (400g) Gouda cheese, grated

1 tblsp cornflour

2 tblsp water

1 wholemeal french loaf

A traditional Swiss Fondue is made with Gruyère cheese but this recipe uses more economical Gouda. Also, white wine only is used but you can make it more 'powerful' by using gin or kirsch instead of the water.

1. Rub the inside of a 2pt (1.2l) glass or pottery mixing bowl with the cut side of the garlic. Pour in the wine and lemon juice.
2. Cook, uncovered, on FULL POWER for 1 minute.

3. Remove from the oven and stir in half the cheese.

4. Return to the microwave and cook, uncovered, on FULL POWER for 2 minutes.

5. Stir in remaining cheese and cook on REHEAT for 5 minutes, stirring twice during cooking.

6. Mix cornflour mixture with the water (or alcohol) in a small bowl. Stir cornflour mixture into cheese then cook on FULL POWER for 1 minute.

7. Leave to stand for 3 minutes before serving. Stir once again and serve with cubes of wholemeal french bread, or sticks of celery and carrots.

Savoury Egg and Parsley Crumble

Serves 4

2oz (50g) vegetable fat

1oz (25g) wholemeal flour

¼pt (150ml) skimmed milk

sea salt and freshly-milled black pepper to taste

pinch freshly-grated nutmeg

2 level tblsp chopped parsley

½oz (15g) freshly-grated Parmesan cheese

4 grade 4 eggs, hardboiled and chopped

1oz (25g) wholemeal breadcrumbs

A quick and easy dish to make for a family supper. Serve with Nutmeg Sauce and courgettes and mushrooms fried with garlic and lemon.

1. Place vegetable fat in a 1pt (600ml) glass or pottery casserole. Cook, uncovered, on FULL POWER for 1 minute.

2. Stir in flour then gradually beat in the milk.

3. Cook, uncovered, on FULL POWER for 30 seconds. Stir well then cook on FULL POWER for 2 minutes, stirring well half way through.

4. Beat in the seasoning, nutmeg, parsley, Parmesan cheese and eggs.

5. Spread level then sprinkle breadcrumbs over the top.

6. Cook, uncovered, on REHEAT, for 2½ minutes.

7. Serve with Nutmeg Sauce (page 115).

73

Nutty Mushroom and Stilton Pie

Serves 6

2 tblsp rape seed oil

3 sticks celery, washed and chopped

1 bunch spring onions, washed and chopped into 1in (2.5cm) lengths

9oz (250g) open mushrooms, wiped and thickly-sliced

3 level tblsp wholemeal flour

½pt (300ml) water

sea salt and freshly-milled black pepper to taste

1oz (25g) hazelnuts, chopped

Pastry

4oz (125g) wholemeal flour

pinch of salt

2oz (50g) vegetable fat

2 tblsp cold water

Extra ingredients

3oz (75g) Stilton cheese, crumbled

½ grade 4 egg, beaten

Stilton is traditionally a Christmas cheese and this pie is ideal for the festive celebrations with a crunchy green salad or even coleslaw.

1. Put oil, celery, spring onions and mushrooms into a 3½pt (2l) glass or pottery bowl. Cover with cling film, then puncture twice with the tip of a knife.
2. Cook on FULL POWER for 5 minutes.
3. Stir in flour then gradually add the water. Return to the microwave and cook, uncovered, on FULL POWER for a further 3 minutes to thicken the liquid.
4. Add the seasoning and nuts then leave to stand until cool.
5. To make pastry, put flour and salt into a basin. Rub in vegetable fat then stir in water to form a stiff dough.
6. Transfer mushroom mixture to a 9in (23cm) round glass or pottery flan dish then sprinkle with cheese.
7. Roll out pastry then use to cover the pie. Press down lightly over filling.
8. Decorate with pastry leaves made from the trimmings. Brush with beaten egg then cook on FULL POWER for 8 minutes.
9. Serve hot or cold.

Serves 4

½oz (15g) vegetable fat

4oz (125g) button mushrooms, wiped clean and finely chopped

1 tblsp flour

4oz (125g) tomatoes, peeled and finely chopped

4oz (125g) cottage cheese

sea salt and freshly-milled black pepper

8oz (225g) chopped frozen spinach, thawed

½oz (15g) vegetable fat, melted

4 grade 4 eggs, separated

large pinch freshly-grated nutmeg

a little freshly-grated Parmesan cheese

Fluffy Spinach Omelette

A sumptuous stuffed omelette packed with a cottage cheese and vegetable filling. Baby boiled potatoes make an ideal accompaniment.

1. Grease a 9in (23cm) glass or pottery quiche dish. Base-line with non-stick parchment paper.
2. Put vegetable fat and mushrooms in a 2pt (1.2l) glass or pottery mixing bowl. Cover with cling film and puncture twice with the tip of a knife.
3. Cook on FULL POWER for 2 minutes.
4. Stir in flour, chopped tomatoes, cottage cheese and seasoning. Cover with a plate.
5. Cook on FULL POWER for 2 minutes, stirring half way through cooking. Keep covered and leave to stand temporarily.
6. Mix spinach, vegetable fat, egg yolks, nutmeg and seasoning together.
7. Whisk egg whites until stiff then fold into spinach mixture.
8. Turn into prepared quiche dish.
9. Cook, uncovered, on ROAST for 5 minutes. Have ready a piece of grease-proof paper sprinkled with Parmesan cheese.
10. Turn spinach omelette out on to paper, then place mushroom mixture on to one half. Quickly flip the other half up and over filling. Cut into 4 portions and serve immediately.

Curried Cheese Tart

Serves 6

Pastry

4oz (125g) wholemeal flour

2oz (50g) vegetable fat

2 tblsp cold water

½ grade 4 egg, beaten

Filling

1 tblsp safflower oil

3oz (75g) red pepper, seeds removed and cut into thin strips

1 level tblsp mango chutney

5oz (150g) Red Leicester cheese, grated

2oz (50g) walnuts, chopped

1 level tsp curry powder

2 grade 3 eggs, beaten

¼pt (150ml) single cream

2 level tblsp chopped parsley

Lightly sweetened with mango chutney, the savoury tart is equally good hot or cold and is ideal for picnics and packed lunches.

1. To make pastry, sift flour into a bowl and rub in fat until mixture resembles fine breadcrumbs. Add water and fork-stir to a firm dough.
2. Roll out fairly thinly on a floured surface and use to line a shallow 8in (20cm) flan dish. Prick well all over, especially where the sides meet the base. Line with kitchen paper and cook, uncovered, on FULL POWER for 6 minutes.
3. Remove from oven and lift out paper. Brush pastry with beaten egg to seal holes. Return to microwave and cook on FULL POWER for a further minute. Leave to cool.
4. For filling, place oil in a small glass or pottery dish with the red pepper. Cover with cling film and puncture twice with the tip of a knife. Cook on FULL POWER for 3 minutes.
5. Spread mango chutney over pastry base.
6. Mix together cheese, nuts, curry powder, eggs and cream. Stir into cooked red pepper. Pour into cooked pastry case and sprinkle with parsley.
7. Cook on FULL POWER for 4 to 5 minutes, or until the centre is lightly set. Leave to stand for a further 4 minutes before serving.

VEGETABLES

The microwave and vegetables are a superb team and whether it's roots, tubers and greens, or even asparagus and peppers, all vegetables retain their natural colour, nutritive values, flavours and firmness when cooked in the microwave. There are some 43 recipes in this section from which to choose starters and main courses and cover dishes such as Potato and Pizza Flan, Caerphilly and Nut Stuffed Peppers, Curried Avocado and Port, Cauliflower Polonaise, Swiss-Style Rösti Potatoes, Baked Plantain, Stuffed Aubergines, Moussaka, Vegetable Pâté and Vegetarian Kebabs. Temptations galore!

Asparagus and Cheese Flan

Serves 6

4oz (125g) wholemeal flour
2oz (50g) vegetable fat
2 tblsp cold water
½ grade 4 egg, beaten
Filling
12oz (350g) fresh asparagus
½pt (275ml) soured cream
2 grade 4 eggs, beaten
4oz (125g) Vegetarian Cheddar cheese, grated
sea salt and freshly-milled black pepper

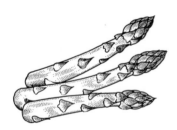

This is a very pretty flan which does full justice to luxury asparagus.

1. To make pastry, sift flour into a bowl then rub in fat until it resembles fine breadcrumbs. Add water and mix to a firm dough by stirring with a fork.

2. Roll out pastry on a floured surface and use to line an 8in (20cm) glass or pottery flan dish. Prick well all over, especially where the sides meet the base. Rest for ½ hour in the refrigerator.

3. Line the flan with kitchen paper and cook, uncovered, on FULL POWER for 6 minutes.

4. Remove from oven and take off kitchen paper. Brush with the beaten egg to seal the holes. Return to the microwave oven and cook on FULL POWER for a further minute. Leave to cool.

5. Trim 6 asparagus spears to about 3½in (20cm) lengths and set aside for decoration.

6. Chop trimmings and the remaining asparagus spears into 1in (2.5cm) lengths, discarding any woody bits at the ends.

7. Put asparagus in a shallow 8in (20cm) glass or pottery dish, placing the 6 special spears on top. Pour over enough boiling water to cover.

8. Cover the dish with cling film, puncture the top twice with the tip of a knife. Cook on FULL POWER for 3 minutes and stand for 2 minutes. Carefully remove the 6 special spears with a slotted spoon. Drain remaining asparagus and cool.

9. In a bowl, beat together the soured cream, eggs, grated cheese and seasoning.

10. Sprinkle the cut asparagus over the base of the cooked flan. Pour over the egg mixture and arrange the special asparagus spears in a pattern like the spokes of a wheel in the centre of the flan.

11. Cook, uncovered, on FULL POWER for 6 minutes. Stand for 3 minutes.

Variation

Follow steps 1-5 then add one finely chopped onion to the chopped asparagus trimmings. Continue steps 7-8. Then reduce cheese in step 9 to 2oz (50g). Complete as per remaining instructions.

Parsley and Lemon Cabbage

Serves 4-6

1½oz (40g) vegetable fat

2 large garlic cloves, crushed

grated rind 1 large lemon

3 level tblsp chopped parsley

2 level tsp mustard seed

1¾lb (800g) green cabbage, finely shredded

2 tblsp cold water

sea salt and freshly-milled black pepper

If you want to make ordinary green cabbage interesting enough to serve at a formal dinner party, then follow this easy recipe. For those who like vegetables crisp in texture, leave the casserole covered for 3 minutes only after cooking.

1. Put vegetable fat, garlic, lemon rind, parsley, mustard seed and cabbage into a 3pt (1.75l) glass or pottery casserole. Sprinkle water over the top. Cover with a matching lid or plate.

2. Cook on FULL POWER for 5 minutes, stirring well 3 times during cooking.

3. Season and stir well. Re-cover and cook on FULL POWER for 1 minute. Keep covered and leave to stand for 3-5 minutes.

Cauliflower Polonaise

Serves 4

1 medium-sized cauliflower

2 tblsp safflower oil

3oz (75g) onion, peeled and finely chopped

2oz (50g) wholemeal flour

1pt (600ml) skimmed milk

6oz (175g) Red Leicester cheese, grated

2 tsp lemon juice

2 level tblsp chopped parsley or dill

6oz (175g) blanched tomatoes, peeled and chopped

2oz (50g) brown breadcrumbs

2 hard boiled eggs, shelled

An innovative dish, supposedly Polish in origin, which is an up-market version of Cauliflower Cheese. It makes an unusual lunch or supper main course.

1. Prepare cauliflower by removing stalk and leaves. Place in a 3½pt (2l) glass or pottery dish with 4 tablespoons hot water. Cover with cling film then puncture twice with the tip of a knife.

2. Cook on FULL POWER for 10 minutes, turning cauliflower over once during cooking. Leave to stand for 10 minutes then transfer to a shallow round 9in (23cm) glass or pottery dish.

3. Place oil into a 2pt (1.2l) glass mixing bowl, add onion and fry on FULL POWER for 3 minutes. Stir in flour then gradually add milk. Cover with lid or plate.

4. Return to microwave and cook on FULL POWER for 5 minutes, stirring twice during cooking.

5. Add cheese and stir until melted. Mix in lemon juice, parsley and tomatoes. Pour over cauliflower.

6. Garnish with lines of breadcrumbs, chopped egg white and sieved egg yolk (both of which can be prepared ahead).

7. Serve hot.

Above: Stuffed Aubergines (p 81)
(Photo: British Alcan)

Below: Cheese and Potato Layer Pie (p 72)
(Photo: English Country Cheese Council)

Stuffed Aubergines

Serves 4

2 small or 1 large aubergine
1 tblsp walnut oil
8oz (225g) onion, finely chopped
2 cloves garlic, crushed
3oz (75g) fresh brown breadcrumbs
6oz (175g) tomatoes, peeled and coarsely chopped
6oz (150g) cup mushrooms
3oz (75g) cashew nuts
12 basil leaves
1 level tsp tomato purée
sea salt and freshly-milled black pepper to taste
4 level tsp grated Parmesan cheese

A Mediterranean speciality, this version is enhanced with walnut oil and cashew nuts.

1. Slit the skin of the aubergines lengthwise all the way round. Place on a large glass or pottery plate, cover with cling film and puncture twice with the tip of a knife. Cook on FULL POWER for 3 minutes and allow to stand for 5 minutes.

2. Put oil, onions and garlic into a 3pt (1.75l) glass or pottery bowl. Cover with cling film and puncture twice with the tip of a knife. Cook on FULL POWER for 2 minutes.

3. Add the breadcrumbs to the onion mixture.

4. Cut the aubergines in half horizontally along the previously split skin. With a metal spoon, carefully remove the pulp and reserve. Arrange the aubergine shells on a 9½in (24cm) shallow glass or pottery dish.

5. Put the aubergine pulp, tomatoes, mushrooms, cashew nuts and basil leaves into a food processor or blender and blend coarsely.

6. Mix the blended vegetables with the onion and breadcrumb mixture. Add the tomato purée and mix very well with a wooden spoon. Season with sea salt and black pepper.

7. Spoon the stuffing mixture carefully into the aubergine shells and sprinkle with the Parmesan cheese. Cover with cling film and puncture twice with the tip of a knife. Cook on FULL POWER for 3 minutes.

8. Serve hot with Balkan Tomato Sauce (page 118).

Mixed Vegetable Casserole with Nut Dumplings (p 43)
(Photo: Corning Microwave Cookware Collection)

Beetroot with Shredded Red Cabbage

Serves 4-6

1lb (450g) red cabbage, finely shredded

6oz (175g) onion, thinly sliced

10 juniper berries, crushed

¼pt (150ml) red wine

8oz (225g) cooked beetroot, coarsely chopped

6oz (175g) carrots, grated

sea salt and freshly-milled black pepper

A glowing red vegetable accompaniment with a subtle tinge of spice. It goes well with strong cheese dishes.

1. Put cabbage, onion, juniper berries and red wine into a 3½pt (2l) glass or pottery casserole. Cover with a matching lid or plate.
2. Cook on FULL POWER for 7 minutes, stirring twice during cooking.
3. Stir in beetroot, carrots and seasoning. Cover with lid.
4. Cook on FULL POWER for 1 minute. Stir round and serve.

Curried Avocado and Port

Serves 4

1oz (25g) butter

2oz (50g) onion, peeled and finely chopped

4 tblsp port

¼ level tsp mild curry powder

1 level tsp fresh mixed herbs

1 level tsp tomato purée

2 medium avocados, stones removed, peeled and sliced

Hot avocados are unusual but they make an excellent starter on a cold evening.

1. Melt butter in a small glass or pottery dish on FULL POWER for ½ minute. Add onion and cook, uncovered, on FULL POWER for 3 minutes.
2. In a 2pt (1.2l) glass or pottery bowl, blend together the port, curry powder, mixed herbs and tomato purée.

3. Add the cooked onion and finely sliced avocados to the curry and port mixture. Stir gently with a wooden spoon to coat the avocados.

4. Divide the mixture between 4 small glass or pottery ramekin dishes. Cover each dish with cling film and puncture twice with the tip of a knife.

5. Cook on REHEAT for 4 minutes. Remove cling film and serve.

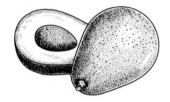

Serves 4

2 tblsp rape seed oil

4oz (125g) onion, peeled and finely chopped

1 small cauliflower, washed and divided into small florets

8oz (225g) french beans, topped and tailed

1 level tsp ground cumin

½ level tsp fresh root ginger, grated

½ level tsp ground turmeric

2oz (50g) split blanched almonds

4 tblsp water

sea salt and freshly-milled black pepper to taste

Curried Cauliflower and Beans

A versatile dish that can be served hot or cold. It goes well with a dish of yogurt topped with chopped, fresh coriander. Also Greek-style sesame seed bread.

1. Place oil, onion, cauliflower, beans, spices and almonds into a 3½pt (2l) glass or pottery dish. Cover with a matching lid or cling film punctured twice with the tip of a knife.

2. Cook on FULL POWER for 3 minutes.

3. Add water and seasoning; stir well and return to microwave. Re-cover as above.

4. Continue to cook for a further 10 minutes or until the cauliflower is tender. Stir frequently during cooking to get the full benefit of the spices.

5. Leave to stand for 8 minutes before serving.

Stuffed Cabbage

Serves 6

2oz (50g) brown rice

1pt (600ml) boiling water

6 large cabbage leaves

½pt (300ml) boiling water

2oz (50g) fresh brown breadcrumbs

4oz (125g) grated Vegetarian Cheddar cheese

1oz (25g) grated Parmesan cheese

4 level tblsp chopped fresh coriander leaves or 1 level tblsp dried coriander leaves (see page 00)

1 tblsp groundnut oil

3 sticks celery, finely chopped

2oz (50g) onion, finely chopped

2 cloves of garlic, crushed

1 grade 3 egg at room temperature, beaten

6 level tsp grated Parmesan cheese

Stuffed cabbage leaves, delicately flavoured with coriander, make a splendid meal starter when served hot with Cumberland Sauce.

1. Put rice into a 3pt (1.75l) glass or pottery bowl and pour over the 1pt (600ml) boiling water. Cover with cling film and puncture twice with the tip of a knife. Cook on FULL POWER for 20 minutes, remove from the oven and leave to stand for 5 minutes.

2. Put the cabbage leaves into another 3pt (1.75l) glass or pottery bowl and pour over the ½pt (300ml) boiling water. Cover with cling film and puncture twice with the tip of a knife. Cook on FULL POWER for 2 minutes.

3. Strain the rice and return to the bowl. Add the breadcrumbs, both cheeses and coriander.

4. Put the oil into a 1pt (600ml) glass or pottery bowl and cook, uncovered, on FULL POWER for 1 minute. Add the celery, onion and garlic. Mix well and cook, uncovered, on FULL POWER for 3 minutes until softened.

5. Add the celery and onion mixture to the rice and breadcrumb mixture.

6. Stir in the beaten egg and mix well.

7. Drain the cabbage leaves. Top centres with equal amounts of rice mixture then fold up like parcels. Arrange in a 9½in (24cm) glass or pottery flan dish with joins underneath. Sprinkle with Parmesan cheese.

8. Cover cabbage parcels with cling film and puncture twice with the top of a knife. Cook on FULL POWER for 5 minutes.

9. Serve with Cumberland Sauce (page 119).

Serves 6

Pastry

4oz (125g) wheatmeal flour

2oz (50g) vegetable fat

2 tblsp cold water

½ grade 4 egg, beaten

Filling

1lb (450g) blanched red tomatoes, peeled and sliced

4oz (125g) courgettes, unpeeled and thinly sliced

4oz (125g) mange tout, topped and tailed then sliced

2 grade 3 eggs, beaten

¼pt (150ml) single cream

1 level tblsp chopped parsley

1 level tsp scissor-snipped chives

1 level tsp chopped fresh sage or large pinch of dried sage

sea salt and freshly-milled black pepper to taste

Courgette, Mange Tout and Tomato Tart

An elegant summer flan designed for entertaining.

1. To make pastry, sift flour into a bowl then rub in fat until mixture resembles fine breadcrumbs. Add water and mix to a firm dough with a fork.

2. Roll out pastry on a floured surface and use to line an 8in (20cm) flan dish. Prick well all over especially where the sides meet the base. Line with kitchen paper and cook, uncovered, on FULL POWER for 6 minutes.

3. Remove from oven and take out kitchen paper. Brush with beaten egg to seal holes. Return to microwave and cook, uncovered, on FULL POWER for a further minute. Leave to cool.

4. Arrange tomatoes, courgettes and mange tout in the flan case.

5. Beat together the eggs, cream, parsley, chives, sage and seasoning. Pour into flan case.

6. Cook, uncovered, on FULL POWER for 8 minutes. Leave to stand for 10 minutes before serving.

Shredded Red Cabbage with Bramley Apples

Serves 4-6

1lb (450g) red cabbage, finely shredded

6oz (175g) onion, thinly sliced

1 tblsp cider vinegar

¼pt (150ml) strong, dry cider

2 level tsp mustard seed

12oz (350g) Bramley apples, peeled, cored and sliced

2 level tblsp soft brown sugar (optional)

sea salt and freshly-milled black pepper to taste

An intoxicating mix to serve with nut loaves and egg dishes.

1. Put cabbage, onion, vinegar, cider and mustard seed into a 3½pt (2 l) glass or pottery casserole. Cover with matching lid or plate.
2. Cook on FULL POWER for 4 minutes, stirring half way through cooking.
3. Stir in remaining ingredients. Re-cover and cook on FULL POWER for 5 minutes, stirring half way through cooking. Keep covered and leave to stand for 3 minutes.

Courgette and Gruyère Cheese Puff

Serves 4

¾oz (20g) vegetable fat

12oz (350g) courgettes, sliced

2 level tblsp flour

¼pt (150ml) skimmed milk

1 level tblsp whole grain mustard

sea salt and freshly-milled black pepper to taste

4oz (125g) Gruyère cheese, grated

2 grade 4 eggs, separated

A wonderfully light, summery supper dish. Serve with jacket potatoes and a salad made from tomatoes and Chinese leaves tossed in a well-flavoured dressing.

1. Put vegetable fat and courgettes into a 2pt (1.2l) glass or pottery casserole. Cover with matching lid or plate.

2. Cook on FULL POWER for 3 minutes, stirring half way through.

3. Stir in flour then gradually blend in milk. Mix in mustard and seasoning. Cover.

4. Cook on FULL POWER for 3 minutes, stirring well after each minute.

5. Stir in cheese and egg yolks. Mix well.

6. Whisk egg whites until stiff then fold into mixture.

7. Cook, uncovered, on ROAST for 5 minutes. Serve immediately.

Baked Plantain

Serves 4

2 large plantain

3 tblsp groundnut oil

1 level tsp sea salt

Plantain makes an excellent accompaniment to any West Indian meal and is an interesting substitute for potatoes.

1. Peel the plantain and cut into large 'chips'.

2. Put oil and salt on to a browning dish and heat on FULL POWER according to the manufacturer's instructions.

3. Remove from the oven and add plantain. Stir well to ensure the 'chips' are coated with oil. Cook, uncovered, on FULL POWER for 1 minute; remove from oven and stir well, return to oven and cook on FULL POWER for further 1 minute; repeat this process 3 more times.

Variation
To serve plantain as a pudding, slice the peeled plantain into ¼in (5mm) 'chunks'. Cook on FULL POWER in the same way as above but omit the salt. Serve sprinkled with sugar and lemon juice.

Avocado and Tomato Flan

Serves 4-6

Pastry

4oz (125g) plain wholemeal flour

pinch cayenne pepper

2oz (50g) vegetable fat

2 tblsp cold water

½ grade 3 egg, beaten

Filling

1 large avocado, halved, stone removed and peeled

3 tblsp lemon juice

8oz (225g) halved cherry tomatoes or 3 large tomatoes, cut into wedges

2 grade 4 eggs, beaten

10oz (275g) fromage frais

sea salt and freshly-milled black pepper to taste

A tasty flan of hot avocado in a delicate creamy sauce. If liked, serve small wedges of flan with a simple garnish of watercress for a first course.

1. To make pastry, sift flour and cayenne pepper into a bowl and rub in fat until it resembles fine breadcrumbs. Add water and fork-mix to a firm dough.

2. Roll out pastry on a floured surface and use to line an 8in (20cm) glass or pottery flan dish. Prick well all over, especially where the sides meet the base. Rest flan for ½ hour in the refrigerator.

3. Line the flan with kitchen paper and cook, uncovered, on FULL POWER for 6 minutes.

4. Remove from oven and take off kitchen paper. Brush with the beaten half egg to seal the holes. Return to the microwave and cook on FULL POWER for a further minute. Leave to cool.

5. Slice avocado, then sprinkle with lemon juice. Arrange, with tomatoes, in flan case.

6. Beat eggs, any remaining lemon juice, fromage frais and seasoning together. Pour into flan.

7. Cover with cling film and puncture twice with the tip of a knife.

8. Cook on ROAST for 7 minutes. Keep covered and leave to stand for 3 minutes. Serve hot or cold in wedges and accompany with a lettuce salad tossed in a sharpish french dressing.

Courgette, Baby Beet and Tomato Crumble

Serves 4

1oz (25g) vegetable fat

10oz (275g) courgettes, sliced

12oz (350g) runner beans, thinly sliced into diagonal strips

8oz (225g) blanched tomatoes, peeled and coarsely chopped

3 level tblsp flour

1 level tsp paprika

½ level tsp vegetable stock extract

¾pt (450ml) hot water

3 bay leaves

¼ level tsp celery salt

sea salt and freshly-milled black pepper to taste

12oz (350g) jar baby beets in sweet vinegar

Crumble topping

1oz (25g) vegetable fat

1oz (25g) sesame seeds

2oz (50g) wheatgerm

2oz (50g) macadamia or brazil nuts, chopped

A tasty and appetising main course topped with a sesame seed and nut crumble. It is at its best accompanied with creamed swede plus minty petits pois mixed with tiny pearl onions.

1. Put vegetable fat and vegetables except baby beets into a 3pt (1.75l) glass or pottery casserole. Cover with a matching lid or plate.
2. Cook on FULL POWER for 3 minutes.
3. Stir in flour and paprika. Dissolve vegetable stock extract in the hot water. Gradually stir into vegetables. Add bay leaves and seasoning. Re-cover.
4. Cook on FULL POWER for 6 minutes, stirring well every 2 minutes. Stir in drained baby beets. Continue cooking for a further 5 minutes. Keep covered and leave to stand temporarily.
5. For crumble, place vegetable fat in a 1pt (600ml) glass or pottery mixing bowl.
6. Cook, uncovered, on FULL POWER for 30 seconds. Stir in remaining ingredients and mix well.
7. Remove bay leaves from casserole. Sprinkle crumble over vegetables.
8. Cook, uncovered, for 2 minutes. Stand 1 minute before serving.

Cauliflower and Tomato Mozarella Flan

Serves 6-8

Pastry

6oz (175g) malted
wheatmeal flour

3oz (75g) vegetable fat

3 tblsp cold water

½ grade 4 egg, beaten

Filling

1oz (25g) vegetable fat

8oz (225g) cauliflower,
divided into tiny florets

1oz (25g) flour

scant ½pt (275ml) skimmed
milk

4oz (125g) tomatoes, peeled
and chopped

2 level tblsp scissor-snipped
chives

2 grade 4 eggs, beaten

sea salt and freshly-milled
black pepper to taste

4oz (125g) Mozarella cheese,
thinly sliced

To garnish

6 to 8 stuffed olives, sliced

A cauliflower cheese flan which owes much to the flavours of Italy. Serve hot or cold.

1. To make pastry, sift flour into bowl, add fat and rub in finely until mixture resembles fine breadcrumbs. Add water and mix to a firm dough with a fork.

2. Turn out on to a floured surface, roll out fairly thinly and use to line a 9in (23cm) glass or pottery flan dish. Prick well all over, especially where the sides meet the base. Rest for ½ hour in the refrigerator.

3. Line with kitchen paper and cook uncovered on FULL POWER for 6 minutes.

4. Remove from oven and take out kitchen paper. Brush pastry with beaten egg to seal holes. Return to the microwave oven and cook on FULL POWER, uncovered, for a further minute. Leave to cool.

5. Place vegetable fat and cauliflower in a 2pt (1.2l) glass or pottery mixing bowl. Cover with cling film and puncture twice with the tip of a knife.

6. Cook on FULL POWER for 3 minutes, lifting film and stirring half way through.

7. Stir in flour then gradually blend in milk, tomatoes and chives. Cover with a plate then cook on FULL POWER for 4 minutes, stirring well after each minute.

8. Beat eggs and seasoning. Pour into flan case. Arrange Mozarella on top.

90

9. Cook, uncovered, on ROAST for 5 minutes. Leave to stand for 4 minutes. Garnish with olives and serve hot or cold.

Serves 4

Stuffing

½oz (15g) vegetable fat

2oz (50g) button mushrooms, wiped clean and finely chopped

2oz (50g) wholemeal breadcrumbs

1 level tblsp scissor-snipped chives

4 fresh sage leaves, finely chopped

1oz (25g) hazelnuts, very finely chopped

1oz (25g) pine nuts

grated rind and juice of ½ lemon

sea salt and freshly-milled black pepper to taste

2 large ripe avocados

Hot Avocado with Nutty Mushroom Stuffing

An unusual starter for four people or a more substantial main meal for two. Although the stuffing may be made ahead of time, do not fill avocados until you are ready to cook them and then serve immediately.

1. Place vegetable fat and mushrooms into a 2pt (1.2l) glass or pottery mixing bowl. Cover with cling film and puncture twice with the tip of a knife.

2. Cook on FULL POWER for 2 minutes.

3. Stir in breadcrumbs, herbs, nuts, lemon rind and seasoning. Mix well.

4. Halve avocados lengthways and remove stones. Place in a large glass or pottery dish. Sprinkle liberally with lemon juice.

5. Pile nut mixture into the cavities of the avocados. Cover with cling film and puncture twice with the tip of a knife.

6. Cook on FULL POWER for 2½ minutes. Serve immediately.

91

Potato Pizza Flan

Serves 6

1lb (450g) potatoes

4 tblsp water

1 grade 3 egg, beaten

1oz (25g) vegetable fat

1 level tsp freshly-grated nutmeg

sea salt and freshly-milled black pepper to taste

1 tblsp rape seed oil

8oz (225g) tomatoes, peeled and chopped

2oz (50g) carrot, sliced

3oz (75g) onion, peeled and sliced

selection of fresh herbs, chopped (approx 1 tsp)

1 clove garlic, crushed

3oz Red Leicester cheese, grated

6 black olives to garnish

An innovative pizza with a potato base and mixed vegetable topping.

1. Slice potatoes; large ones into 16 pieces, smaller ones into 8. Place in a 1pt (600ml) glass or pottery dish with 4 tablespoons water. Cover with cling film then puncture twice with the tip of a knife. Cook on FULL POWER for 10 minutes or until tender. Leave to stand for 5 minutes.

2. Drain potatoes, then purée in a blender or food processor with the egg, vegetable fat, nutmeg and seasoning.

3. Press potato mixture into a well-greased 10in (25cm) pizza plate or shallow dish. Cook, uncovered, on FULL POWER for 8 minutes and leave to stand.

4. Place oil, tomatoes, carrot, onion, herbs and garlic into a bowl. Cover with cling film then puncture twice with the tip of a knife. Cook on FULL POWER for 8 minutes, lifting film and stirring twice while cooking.

5. Spoon vegetable mixture on top of potato base. Sprinkle with cheese and garnish with olives.

6. Cook, uncovered, on REHEAT for 3 minutes. Serve with a fresh green salad.

Swiss-Style Rösti Potatoes

Serves 2

12oz (350g) potatoes

2 tblsp sunflower oil

sea salt

This rösti-type potato cake is an excellent accompaniment to egg and cheese dishes.

1. Peel potatoes and slice very thinly into strips with a potato peeler. Put potatoes into a 3pt (1.75l) bowl and cover with boiling water. Leave for 2 minutes then drain. Wipe dry in a tea towel.

2. Put oil on to a browning dish and heat on FULL POWER in the microwave according to manufacturer's instructions (usually 5 minutes).

3. Spread the potato slices over the browning dish and press down well. Cook on FULL POWER for 3 minutes.

4. Remove from the oven and turn the potatoes over, using a fish slice. Press down well. Return to the oven and cook on FULL POWER for a further 3 minutes.

5. Season with the salt and serve.

Crumbed Potatoes with Parmesan and Chives

Serves 4

1½lb (750g) potatoes, peeled and cut into ½in (1cm) cubes

1½oz (40g) vegetable fat

sea salt and freshly-milled black pepper to taste

1½oz (40g) granary breadcrumbs

2 level tblsp freshly-grated Parmesan cheese

1½ level tblsp scissor-snipped chives

Crumbed potatoes are delicious and go well with all manner of main courses based on egg, cheese and mixed vegetables.

1. Put potatoes and vegetable fat into a 2pt (1.2l) glass or pottery oven dish. Cover with cling film and puncture twice with the tip of a knife.

2. Cook on FULL POWER for 6 minutes, lifting film and stirring at half time.

3. Stir in seasoning. Mix remaining ingredients together then sprinkle over potato.

4. Cook, uncovered, on FULL POWER for 2 minutes.

Serves 6

1oz (25g) vegetable fat

5oz (150g) red pepper, seeds removed and finely chopped

4oz (125g) green pepper, seeds removed and finely chopped

2 cloves garlic, crushed

2oz (50g) cup mushrooms, wiped clean and finely chopped

3 level tblsp flour

¼ level tsp vegetable stock extract

½pt (300ml) hot water

1 tblsp Worcestershire sauce

1 level tblsp whole grain mustard

sea salt and freshly-milled black pepper to taste

2 level tblsp wholemeal breadcrumbs

2 level tblsp pumpkin seeds

Mixed Pepper and Pumpkin Ramekins

Flavoursome ingredients combine to make this meal starter something quite special.

1. Put vegetable fat in a 2pt (1.2l) glass or pottery mixing bowl with peppers and garlic. Cover with lid or plate.
2. Cook on FULL POWER for 2 minutes. Stir in mushrooms. Re-cover.
3. Cook on FULL POWER for 1 minute.
4. Stir in flour. Dissolve vegetable stock extract in the hot water and then gradually stir into vegetables with Worcestershire sauce, mustard and seasoning.
5. Re-cover with lid or plate. Cook on FULL POWER for 4 minutes, stirring well after each minute.
6. Divide filling between 6 glass or pottery ramekin dishes.
7. Mix breadcrumbs and pumpkin seeds together. Sprinkle over ramekins.
8. Cook, uncovered, on REHEAT for 2 minutes.

Serves 4

2oz (50g) margarine

2lb (900g) potatoes, washed and cut into ½in (1.25cm) dice

Potato and Runner Bean Bake

A bountiful main course laced with apple juice. It should be served with poached or scrambled eggs.

sea salt and freshly-milled black pepper to taste

8oz (225g) topped and tailed runner beans, sliced

4oz (125g) mushrooms, sliced

2 tblsp apple juice

1oz (25g) freshly-grated Parmesan cheese

2oz (50g) fresh wholemeal breadcrumbs

1. Place margarine, potatoes and seasoning in a 3½pt (2l) glass or pottery dish. Cover with cling film, then puncture twice with the tip of a knife.

2. Cook on FULL POWER for 10 minutes, lifting film and stirring twice.

3. Add beans, mushrooms and apple juice. Re-cover and cook on FULL POWER for 5 minutes.

4. Sprinkle with cheese and breadcrumbs. Leave uncovered and cook on FULL POWER for a further 7 minutes.

5. Serve hot as a main dish or cold as part of a salad.

Serves 4

2 green pawpaw

½pt (300ml) cold water

2 tblsp groundnut oil

3oz (75g) onion, chopped

1 clove garlic, crushed

4oz (125g) green pepper, de-seeded and sliced

2oz (50g) tomato, peeled and chopped

sea salt and freshly-milled black pepper to taste

2oz (50g) fresh brown breadcrumbs

Baked Pawpaw

An exotic vegetable, given the African treatment. Serve it with pasta and rice dishes.

1. Peel the pawpaw, cut in half lengthways and remove seeds. Cut flesh into chunks. Put the chunks into a 3pt (1.75l) glass or pottery bowl and add the water. Cover with cling film and puncture twice with the tip of a knife. Cook on FULL POWER for 9 minutes.

2. Put oil into a 3pt (1.75l) glass or pottery bowl. Add the onion, the garlic, green pepper and tomato. Stir well, cover with a lid or plate and cook on FULL POWER for 3 minutes.

3. Strain the pawpaw and add to the onion mixture. Season with the salt and pepper and stir well. Transfer to a 2pt (1.2l) glass or pottery shallow serving dish, sprinkle with breadcrumbs and cook, uncovered, on FULL POWER for 8 minutes.

Chicory with Celery and Red Leicester Sauce

Serves 4

1oz (25g) vegetable fat

2 large sticks celery, chopped

2 level tblsp flour

½pt (300ml) skimmed milk

4oz (125g) Red Leicester cheese, grated

sea salt and freshly-milled black pepper to taste

3 × 4oz (125g) heads of chicory, each cut in half lengthways

1 × 5oz (150g) blanched tomato, peeled and sliced

1oz (25g) pumpkin seeds

A pleasant supper dish using two of winter's crispest vegetable: chicory and celery. Accompany with granary rolls for good health.

1. Put vegetable fat into a 2pt (1.2l) glass or pottery mixing bowl with celery. Cover with cling film and puncture twice with the tip of a knife.

2. Cook on FULL POWER for 3 minutes.

3. Uncover, stir in flour then gradually blend in milk. Re-cover with a lid or plate.

4. Cook on FULL POWER for 4 minutes, stirring well after each minute.

5. Add cheese and seasoning and mix in well.

6. Arrange chicory, in a single layer, in a 2in × 8in (5cm × 20cm) round glass dish. Pour cheese and celery sauce over the top. Cover with cling film and puncture twice with the tip of a knife.

7. Cook on FULL POWER for 3 minutes.

8. Arrange tomato slices over chicory, then scatter with pumpkin seeds. Re-cover as before.

9. Cook on FULL POWER for 2 minutes. Keep covered and leave to stand for 1 minute.

Vegetarian Moussaka (p 112)
(Photo: British Alcan)

Stuffed Mushrooms with Sunflower Seeds

Serves 2-4

1½oz (40g) vegetable fat

5oz (150g) green pepper, seeds removed and finely chopped

1 large clove garlic, crushed

4 x 3oz (75g) flat mushrooms, wiped clean

1oz (25g) sunflower seeds

2 level tblsp pine nuts

sea salt and freshly-milled black pepper to taste

An appealing starter for four or main course for two, these stuffed mushrooms are quick to prepare and have a delicious crunch of sunflower seeds and elusive taste of pine nuts.

1. Put vegetable fat into a 2pt (1.2l) glass or pottery mixing bowl with green pepper and garlic. Cover with cling film and puncture twice with the tip of a knife.
2. Cook on FULL POWER for 2 minutes.
3. Finely chop mushroom stalks. Stir into green pepper mixture. Cover with cling film and puncture twice with the tip of a knife.
4. Cook on FULL POWER for 1 minute.
5. Uncover and stir in sunflower seeds, pine nuts and seasoning.
6. Arrange mushrooms on a round glass or pottery serving platter. Divide filling between the mushrooms. Cover with cling film and puncture twice with the tip of a knife.
7. Cook on FULL POWER for 3 minutes. Serve hot.

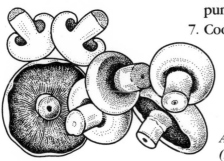

Above: Stuffed Onions (p 105)
(Photo: Kellogg Company of Great Britain Ltd.)

Below: Shredded Red Cabbage with Bramley Apples (p 86)
(Photo: Apple & Pear Development Council)

Serves 4

1lb (450g) potatoes, washed and chopped into pieces; large into 16, small into 8

4 tblsp hot water

2 grade 3 eggs, beaten separately in 2 dishes or bowls

2 tblsp rape seed oil

3oz (75g) onion, peeled and finely chopped

8oz (225g) cup mushrooms, wiped and thinly sliced

2oz (50g) canned sweetcorn kernels

2oz (50g) pine nuts

2oz (50g) Red Leicester cheese

1oz (25g) Caerphilly cheese

sea salt and freshly-milled black pepper to taste

½pt (300ml) skimmed milk

Mushroom and Potato Wedges

A vegetarian version of shepherd's pie, this is a sustaining dish with a mild flavour.

1. Place potatoes in a 3½pt (2l) glass or pottery dish with the hot water. Cover with cling film then puncture twice with the tip of a knife.
2. Cook on FULL POWER for 10 minutes or until the potatoes are just done. Leave to stand for 10 minutes. Purée potatoes in a blender or food processor with 1 beaten egg.
3. Put oil, onion, mushrooms and sweetcorn into a small glass or pottery dish. Cover with cling film, then puncture twice with the tip of a knife. Cook on FULL POWER for 3 minutes.
4. Add all remaining ingredients except puréed potatoes.
5. Turn the vegetable mixture into a 7in (18cm) glass or pottery flan dish. Cover with cling film, then puncture twice with the tip of a knife. Cook on FULL POWER for 6 minutes, then leave to stand for 10 minutes.
6. Cover vegetable mixture with the puréed potato and cook, uncovered, on REHEAT for 5 minutes to set the potato.
7. Serve hot or cold, cut into wedges.

Serves 4

2oz (50g) vegetable fat

8oz (225g) okra, stalks and tips removed, then cut into 1in (2.5cm) pieces

Baked Okra

This is a colourful and unusual side dish. Okra — or ladies fingers as they are sometimes known — is now in our shops most of the year.

6oz (175g) tomatoes, peeled and chopped
3oz (75g) onion, sliced
3oz (75g) red pepper, de-seeded and thinly sliced
4oz (125g) couscous
sea salt and freshly-milled black pepper to taste

1. Melt vegetable fat in a 3½pt (2l) glass or pottery dish on REHEAT for 30 seconds.
2. Add all the remaining ingredients to the dish and mix well.
3. Cook, uncovered, on FULL POWER for 7 minutes. Stir 3 times during the cooking period.
4. Serve hot.

Serves 6
2 corn on the cob
1oz (25g) arame sea weed
3 tblsp Sweet and Sour Sauce (page 116)
2 tblsp soy oil
½ level tsp sea salt
1 clove garlic, crushed
3 sticks of celery, chopped
4oz (125g) Chinese leaves, shredded
4oz (125g) bean sprouts
2oz (50g) water chestnuts, sliced

Stir-Fry Chinese Leaves

An interesting combination of vegetables to accompany any Oriental meal.

1. Put sweetcorn on to a shallow glass or pottery dish or plate and cover with cling film. Puncture twice with the tip of a knife and cook on FULL POWER for 8 minutes. Allow to stand for 5 minutes. Strip kernels from the cob with a knife and set the kernels aside temporarily.
2. Soak the sea weed as directed on the packet.
3. Put Sweet and Sour Sauce, oil, salt and garlic into a 4pt (2.25l) glass or pottery bowl. Heat on FULL POWER for 1 minute.
4. Put all ingredients into the sauce mixture, stir well and cook, uncovered, on FULL POWER for 1 minute.
5. Remove from oven, stir well and return to microwave. Cook on FULL POWER for a further 1 minute; repeat this process twice more.
6. Serve in a shallow 8in (20cm) dish.

Serves 4

4 medium sized potatoes, scrubbed clean

Baked Jacket Potatoes

An old favourite, speedily cooked in the microwave.

1. Line a glass or pottery plate with kitchen paper. Add potatoes and prick all over. Cover with more kitchen paper.
2. Cook on FULL POWER for 8 minutes. Turn each potato once and cook on FULL POWER for a further 8 minutes.
3. Wrap each potato with aluminium foil and allow to stand for 5 minutes.
4. Open the aluminium foil and make a crosscut on top of each potato. Open up by pressing or squeezing base of each potato gently in the hand.

If cooking one potato at a time allow 4 minutes cooking time on FULL POWER, two potatoes = 8 minutes cooking time on FULL POWER, three potatoes = 12 minutes cooking time on FULL POWER.

Variations for 4 potatoes

Top potatoes with any of the following:

1. 4oz (125g) low fat spread mixed with 4oz (125g) grated Vegetarian cheese and 2 level teaspoons whole grain mustard.
2. 4oz (125g) safflower margarine mixed with one peeled and crushed garlic clove and 1 level tablespoon chopped parsley or dill.
3. 4oz (125g) sunflower margarine mixed with 1 level teaspoon creamed horseradish or a squeeze of lemon juice.
4. 4oz (125g) grated Red Leicester cheese mixed with 1 level tablespoon mayonnaise and 1 teaspoon fresh lemon juice.

Potato Pots

Serves 4

12oz (350g) potatoes, washed
and diced

4 tblsp rape seed oil

3oz (75g) medium onion,
chopped

1 tblsp wheatmeal flour

¼pt (150ml) skimmed milk

½ 260g can flageolet beans,
drained

2oz (50g) Vegetarian
Cheddar cheese

sea salt and freshly-milled
black pepper to taste

4 slices wholemeal bread, cut
into 4in (10cm) rounds

1 tomato, quartered

These can be served either as a starter or as a light main meal. A browning dish is necessary to cook the bread which is used as a topping.

1. Put potatoes, half the oil and the onion into a 2pt (1.2l) glass or pottery bowl. Cover with cling film, then puncture twice with the tip of a knife.

2. Cook on FULL POWER for 5 minutes.

3. Remove from microwave and stir in flour. Gradually add the milk, then add the beans, cheese and seasoning.

4. Cover with a lid or plate and cook on FULL POWER for 2 minutes. Stir with a wooden spoon. Use to fill 4 glass or pottery ramekin dishes and set aside.

5. Pour remaining oil over the browning dish and heat on FULL POWER in the microwave according to manufacturer's instructions (usually 5 minutes).

6. Carefully place the rounds of bread on the browning dish and turn in the fat.

7. Cook bread on FULL POWER for 1 minute, turning often, until it is golden brown and crisp.

8. Carefully remove browning dish from oven and place fried bread on top of potato mixture. Return ramekins to the oven and cook, uncovered, on REHEAT for 3 minutes.

9. Serve garnished with tomato.

Spicy Root Vegetable Curry

½pt (300ml) skimmed milk

3oz (75g) desiccated coconut

1½oz (40g) vegetable fat

2 green chillies, seeds removed and finely shredded

3 garlic cloves, crushed

1in (2.5cm) length fresh ginger root, peeled and grated

6oz (175g) onion, finely chopped

2 level tsp ground coriander

1 level tsp ground turmeric

1 level tsp ground cumin

8oz (225g) carrots, sliced

8oz (225g) swedes, diced

4oz (125g) parsnips, diced

4oz (125g) turnips, diced

1 level tblsp cornflour

1 tblsp water

sea salt and freshly-milled black pepper to taste

To garnish

toasted coconut

A pungent and fairly hot vegetable curry which should be served with natural brown rice and side dishes of sliced bananas sprinkled with lemon juice and raisins, toasted almonds, natural yogurt mixed with diced cucumber and mint, toasted coconut and a crisp green salad.

1. Measure milk into a glass jug. Cover with cling film and puncture twice with the tip of a knife.
2. Cook on FULL POWER for 3 minutes.
3. Pour milk on to coconut. Cover and leave on one side temporarily.
4. Put vegetable fat in a 3pt (1.75l) glass or pottery casserole with chillies, garlic, ginger and onion. Cover with a matching lid or plate.
5. Cook on FULL POWER for 1 minute.
6. Stir in spices. Cover and cook on FULL POWER for 2 minutes.
7. Add vegetables and stir until well-coated with spices.
8. Cover and cook on FULL POWER for 2 minutes.
9. Stir in strained milk, squeezing coconut well.
10. Blend cornflour with water until smooth, then stir into casserole with seasoning.
11. Cook on FULL POWER for 13 minutes, stirring 3 times during cooking. Keep covered and leave to stand for 5 minutes. Garnish with toasted coconut.

Mixed Vegetables with Horseradish Crumble

Serves 4-6

1½oz (40g) vegetable fat
8oz (225g) celery, cut into narrow strips
8oz (225g) turnips, cut into narrow strips
12oz (350g) parsnips, cut into narrow strips
4oz (125g) carrots, cut into narrow strips
4oz (125g) onion, finely chopped
2 level tblsp flour
¾pt (450ml) vegetable stock
2 level tblsp grated horseradish OR 3 level tblsp horseradish sauce
sea salt and freshly-milled black pepper to taste

Crumble

1½oz (40g) vegetable fat
2oz (50g) sesame seeds
2oz (50g) wheatgerm
2 level tblsp chopped parsley

A mixture of sesame seeds, wheatgerm and parsley combine together to make an unusual crumble topping for this vegetable medley with delicious, mouth-watering results.

1. Put vegetable fat in a 3½pt (2l) glass or pottery casserole with the vegetables. Cover with a matching lid or plate.
2. Cook on FULL POWER for 6 minutes, stirring 3 times during cooking.
3. Stir in flour. Gradually stir in stock, horseradish and seasoning. Cover.
4. Cook on FULL POWER for 3 minutes, stirring well after each minute. Continue cooking for 12 minutes, stirring twice during cooking. Keep covered and leave on one side temporarily.
5. For crumble, put vegetable fat into a 2pt (1.2l) glass or pottery mixing bowl.
6. Cook, uncovered, on FULL POWER for 1 minute. Stir in the remaining ingredients and mix well. Spoon over vegetables.
7. Cook, uncovered, on FULL POWER for 1 minute. Re-cover, then leave to stand for 5 minutes.

Layered Ratatouille and Dolcelatte

Serves 4

6oz (175g) onion, finely chopped

5oz (150g) green pepper, seeds removed and cut into thin strips

6oz (175g) courgette, sliced

6oz (175g) aubergine, thinly sliced

14oz (400g) can peeled tomatoes, drained and chopped

2 level tblsp tomato purée

sea salt and freshly-milled black pepper

4 to 6oz (125g to 175g) Dolcelatte cheese, sliced

The creamy Dolcelatte melts just enough to reveal some of the colourful courgette and tomato mixture beneath — appealing to the eye and extremely good to eat.

1. Put vegetables into a 3pt (1.75l) glass or pottery mixing bowl with tomato purée and seasoning. Cover with cling film and puncture twice with the tip of a knife.
2. Cook on FULL POWER for 10 minutes, stirring 3 times during cooking.
3. Layer half the ratatouille in a 2pt (1.2l) deep glass or pottery serving dish. Top with half the Dolcelatte. Repeat with a second layer of ratatouille and finally a layer of Dolcelatte. Cover with cling film and puncture twice with the tip of a knife.
4. Cook on ROAST for 1½ minutes. Serve with egg dishes.

Stuffed onions

Serves 4

1 grade 3 egg, beaten

1oz (25g) All-Bran

4 large onions (each 6oz or 175g), peeled

6oz (175g) sorrel or fresh leaf spinach, rinsed and chopped

sea salt and freshly-milled black pepper to taste

Stuffed onions like these, with a high-fibre filling, are healthy and immensely tasty, the ideal accompaniment to egg, rice, bean and pasta dishes.

1. Put half the beaten egg in a small bowl with the All-Bran. Stir and leave aside temporarily.
2. Scoop the centres out of the onions with a grapefruit knife. Reserve. Leave the onion shells about two or three layers thick. Reserve.

4oz (125g) Red Leicester
cheese, grated

To garnish

sprigs of parsley

3. Chop 2oz (50g) of the reserved onion and add to the chopped sorrel or spinach. Stir in the softened bran and egg mixture. Season to taste.

4. Stuff each onion shell with this mixture. (Pack it down firmly as it does sink down further during cooking.)

5. Brush with the remaining beaten egg then arrange the stuffed onions on a large glass plate.

6. Cook, uncovered, on FULL POWER for 10 minutes.

7. Remove from the oven and top the onions with the grated cheese.

8. Return to the microwave and cook on FULL POWER for 1 minute. Leave to stand for 3 minutes before serving.

9. Garnish with parsley.

Serves 4-6

½oz (15g) vegetable fat

12oz (350g) potatoes, grated

12oz (350g) carrrots, grated

6oz (175g) turnips, grated

6oz (175g) swedes, grated

2 level tblsp chopped parsley
and 2 level tsp chopped fresh
thyme, mixed

2 sprigs of mint, chopped

sea salt and freshly-milled
black pepper

Mixed Vegetable and Herb Cake

A most attractive-looking layered vegetable side dish which goes well with the Creamy Kidney Bean Pancakes (page 30).

1. Line a 6in (15cm) glass or pottery soufflé dish with non-stick parchment. Grease sides with vegetable fat.

2. Fill with alternate layers of vegetables, herbs and seasoning. Press down then cover with cling film. Puncture twice with the tip of a knife.

3. Cook on FULL POWER for 8 minutes. Keep covered and leave to stand for 5 minutes.

4. Stand dish on a serving platter and spoon cake onto warm plates.

Vegetable Pâté

Serves 4-6

6 spring onions, trimmed

8oz (225g) aubergine

8oz (225g) cup mushrooms

2oz (50g) vegetable fat

2oz (50g) fresh brown breadcrumbs

2oz (50g) mixed nuts, e.g. cashew and peanut

3oz (75g) Vegetarian Cheddar cheese

4oz (125g) skimmed milk soft cheese (Quark)

sea salt and freshly-milled black pepper

4 tsp cider vinegar or tarragon vinegar

This is a coarse vegetable pâté which should serve six people as a starter or four people for a more substantial lunch.

1. Coarsely chop spring onions, aubergines and mushrooms. Put into a 4pt (2.25l) glass or pottery bowl with the vegetable fat. Cover with cling film and puncture twice with the tip of a knife. Cook on FULL POWER for 6 minutes.
2. Put the breadcrumbs into a 3pt (1.75l) glass or pottery bowl.
3. Coarsely grind the nuts in a food processor or blender and mix with the breadcrumbs.
4. Grate the vegetarian cheese and add to breadcrumb mixture.
5. Using a food processor or blender, blend the cooked vegetables to a coarse purée. Add to the breadcrumb mixture.
6. Stir the soft cheese into the vegetable and breadcrumb mixture. Mix well together with a wooden spoon.
7. Season with the salt, pepper and vinegar.
8. Spread mixture into a shallow 1½pt (900ml) oval dish and chill well.
9. Serve with hot toast or raw vegetables.

Braised Vegetables

Serves 4

12oz (350g) swede, cut into 1in (2.5cm) cubes

8oz (225g) carrots, cut into ½in (1cm) diagonal slices

8oz (225g) parsnip, cut into 1in (2.5cm) pieces

A fast way of cooking winter roots — make a companionable accompaniment to sturdy main courses.

1. Place swede, carrots, parsnips and water into a 3½pt (2l) glass or pottery dish with seasoning. Cover with a plate.

4 tblsp water

sea salt and freshly-milled black pepper

---

2. Cook on FULL POWER for 9 minutes, stirring 3 times. Keep covered and leave to stand for 5 minutes.
3. Drain vegetables and place in a glass or pottery serving dish.

Serves 4

4 x 5oz (150g) green peppers

boiling water

½oz (15g) vegetable fat

4oz (125g) button mushrooms, wiped clean and very finely chopped

1 clove garlic, crushed

5oz (150g) blanched tomatoes, peeled and finely chopped

3oz (75g) wholemeal breadcrumbs

2oz (50g) unblanched almonds, very finely chopped

1oz (25g) brazil nuts, very finely chopped

4oz (125g) Caerphilly cheese, grated

12 black olives, stoned and chopped

sea salt and freshly-milled black pepper to taste

Caerphilly and Nut Stuffed Peppers

Stuffed peppers are always a popular dish and these are especially tasty with their almost Grecian filling of nuts, cheese and black olives.

1. Slice tops off the peppers and discard with the seeds. Place peppers in a 3pt (1.75l) deep glass dish and half fill with boiling water. Cover with cling film and puncture twice with the tip of a knife.
2. Cook on FULL POWER for 3 minutes. Keep covered and leave to stand temporarily.
3. Place vegetable fat in a 2pt (1.2l) glass or pottery mixing bowl with mushrooms and garlic. Cover.
4. Cook on FULL POWER for 2 minutes.
5. Stir in remaining ingredients and mix well. Drain green peppers and fill with Caerphilly and nut mixture. Return to their original dish. Cover with cling film as above.
6. Cook on ROAST for 6 minutes. Keep covered and leave to stand for 3 minutes. Serve hot with a mixed green salad.

Serves 4

4oz (125g) aubergine, wiped
and chopped

8oz (225g) courgettes, sliced

1 small cauliflower, divided
into small florets

4oz (125g) green pepper, de-
seeded and chopped

6oz (175g) carrots, peeled
and sliced

8oz (225g) potatoes, washed
and sliced

1lb (450g) tomatoes, peeled
and chopped

½pt (300ml) dry cider

¼pt (150ml) vegetable stock

3 to 4 level tblsp chopped
parsley

3 level tblsp onion chutney

sea salt and freshly-milled
black pepper to taste

Country Vegetable Hotpot with Cider

Reminiscent of country cottages with roses round the doors, this is a delicious hotpot brewed in West Country cider.

1. Place all the ingredients in a 3½pt (2l) glass or pottery dish. Cover with cling film then puncture twice with the tip of a knife.
2. Cook on FULL POWER for 15 minutes, lifting film and stirring 3 times during cooking with a wooden spoon. Serve with freshly cooked pasta or creamed potatoes.

Serves 4

½oz (15g) vegetable fat

4oz (125g) onion, finely
chopped

1 garlic clove, crushed

2 sticks celery, finely chopped

Chilli Bean Stuffed Dutch Tomatoes

1. Put vegetable fat in a 2pt (1.2l) glass or pottery mixing bowl with onion, garlic, celery and chilli pepper. Cover with cling film and puncture twice with the tip of a knife.

1 red chilli pepper, seeds removed and very finely chopped

7½oz (213g) can red kidney beans, drained and lightly mashed

sea salt and freshly-milled black pepper to taste

4 x 8oz (225g) Dutch tomatoes

2. Cook on FULL POWER for 3 minutes.
3. Stir in mashed kidney beans and seasoning.
4. Slice tops off the tomatoes and scoop out the core and seeds with a teaspoon. Chop 4 tablespoons of the cores and add to kidney bean mixture. (Keep the remainder for making a tomato sauce, soup or adding to any number of recipes.)
5. Divide filling between tomato shells. Arrange in a large glass or pottery dish. Cover with cling film and puncture twice with the tip of a knife.
6. Cook on FULL POWER for 4 minutes. Keep covered and leave to stand for 2 minutes before serving.

Serves 4

8oz (225g) brown rice

1 level tsp sea salt

1pt (600ml) boiling water

3in (7.5cm) stick cucumber, cut into large chunks

8 cherry or small tomatoes

8 button mushrooms

8 black grapes, halved and pips removed

3 tblsp walnut oil

2 tblsp raspberry vinegar

sea salt and freshly-milled black pepper to taste

Vegetarian Kebabs

Kebabs don't always have to be meaty to be served with a barbecue sauce. Here is an alternative.

1. Put rice in a 3½pt (2l) glass or pottery dish with 1 teaspoon salt and 1pt (600ml) boiling water. Cover with cling film, then puncture twice with the tip of a knife.
2. Cook on FULL POWER for 25 minutes. Leave to stand for 10 minutes.
3. Pile rice into a large shallow dish and fluff up with a fork. Cover with foil to keep warm.
4. Thread vegetables and fruit on to 4 wooden kebab skewers.
5. Brush with baste made by whisking together the oil, vinegar and seasoning.
6. Place kebabs on a large plate and cook on FULL POWER for 3 minutes.
7. Serve hot on the bed of rice and accompany with the Barbecue Sauce (page 120). (Use the foil to keep food warm while re-heating the Barbecue Sauce.)

109

Serves 4

Topping

8oz (225g) self raising
wholemeal flour

2oz (50g) vegetable fat

3oz (75g) Red Leicester
cheese, grated

pinch mustard powder

¼pt (150ml) skimmed milk

Vegetable base

2 tblsp rape seed oil

2 sticks celery, chopped

1 clove garlic, crushed

1½oz (40g) wheatmeal flour

¾pt (450ml) skimmed milk

4oz (125g) mature Cheddar
cheese, grated

sea salt and freshly-milled
black pepper to taste

1 level tsp chopped fresh
thyme or ¼ level tsp dried
thyme

1½lb (750g) mixed
vegetables, chopped and
lightly cooked, eg peppers,
courgettes, tomatoes,
sweetcorn, red cabbage,
mushrooms, leeks or any
other vegetables in season

1 tblsp skimmed milk

1 level tblsp poppy seeds

Vegetable Cobbler with Wholemeal Scone Topping

The wholemeal scone topping turns this vegetable dish into a hearty meal for the family.

1. Sift flour into a large bowl, add vegetable fat and rub in finely. Add cheese and mustard. Stir in milk and mix to a soft but not sticky dough with a fork. Cover with cling film and put in the refrigerator for the time being.

2. Put oil, celery and garlic into a large glass or pottery dish. Cover with lid or plate and cook on FULL POWER for 3 minutes.

3. Add flour then gradually stir in the milk. Mix in the cheese, seasoning, thyme and cooked vegetables. Mix well. Cover as above.

4. Cook on FULL POWER for 5 minutes to thicken sauce. Stir once during cooking.

5. Turn vegetable mixture into a 9in (23cm) pie dish.

6. Roll out dough and stamp out 10 rounds using a 2½in (6cm) fluted cutter.

7. Brush the top of each round with a little milk and sprinkle with poppy seeds.

8. Arrange on top of vegetables. Cook on FULL POWER for 10 minutes. Serve immediately.

Spring Vegetable Medley

Serves 4

1 christophene, peeled, quartered, core removed and sliced lengthways

1 small squash, peeled and sliced

4oz (125g) onion, chopped

8oz (225g) tomatoes, peeled and chopped

4oz (125g) okra, topped and tailed

1 small fennel root, trimmed and sliced

¼pt (150ml) water

½ tsp sea salt and freshly-milled black pepper to taste

A mix of unusual vegetables combines to make an excellent side dish for curries, egg dishes or pizza.

1. Prepare all the vegetables and reserve a few fennel leaves for decoration.
2. Arrange vegetables, water and seasoning in a 3pt (1.75l) glass or pottery bowl. Cover with cling film and puncture twice with the tip of a knife. Cook on FULL POWER for 3 minutes.
3. Remove from oven. Take off cling film and stir well. Return to the oven and cook, uncovered, on FULL POWER for further 3 minutes. Remove from the oven and stir.
4. Return to the oven and cook, uncovered, on FULL POWER for further 3 minutes.
5. Remove from the oven and transfer the vegetables, with a perforated spoon, to a heated shallow 8in (20cm) serving dish. Cover with aluminium foil to keep warm.
6. Cook the vegetable liquid on FULL POWER for 5 minutes to reduce the quantity by one-third. Pour reduced vegetable liquid over the cooked vegetables and serve decorated with a few chopped fennel leaves.

Vegetable Moussaka

An unusual version of moussaka; all vegetarian and made with West Indian yams instead of potatoes

Serves 4

1lb (450g) yams, peeled and thinly sliced

4 tblsp cold water

4oz (125g) aubergine, sliced and soaked for ½ hour in salted water

4 tblsp safflower oil

6oz (175g) onion, peeled and sliced

1lb (450g) tomatoes, peeled and sliced

8oz (225g) courgettes, sliced

3oz (75g) green pepper, cored and sliced

sea salt and freshly-milled black pepper to taste

¼pt (150ml) White Sauce (page 114).

1 egg yolk

2 level tblsp Parmesan cheese, grated

1. Place sliced yams in a 3½pt (2l) glass or pottery dish with 4 tablespoons water. Cover with cling film and puncture twice with the tip of a knife.
2. Cook on FULL POWER for 5 minutes then leave to stand for a further 5 minutes. Drain.
3. Meanwhile, in another 3½pt (2l) glass or pottery dish, place the drained aubergines, oil, onion, tomatoes, courgettes, pepper and seasoning. Cover with cling film as before.
4. Cook on FULL POWER for 10 minutes, lifting film and stirring twice during cooking.
5. Fill an 8in (20cm) glass or pottery casserole dish with alternate layers of yams and aubergine mixture, finishing with yams.
6. Make a White Sauce, see page 114. Cool slightly and add the egg yolk.
7. Spread the sauce over the yams and sprinkle with cheese. Cook, uncovered, on FULL POWER for 10 minutes. Leave to stand 3 minutes before serving.

SAUCES

From White to Cumberland; Sweet-Sour to Balkan Tomato; Pineapple and Cider to Nutmeg; Barbecue to Strong Mustard. Just a taster of the kind of sauces in a very comprehensive section with guidelines as to which sauce goes with what dish. A roux, which has been used and mentioned frequently, is the basis of most sauces and is a cooked combination of fat and flour in equal parts.

White Sauce

Makes ½pt (300ml)

½pt (300ml) skimmed milk

1oz (25g) vegetable fat

1oz (25g) plain flour

sea salt and white pepper to taste

1. Pour the skimmed milk into a 1pt (600ml) glass or pottery jug. Cook, uncovered, on FULL POWER for 2 minutes. Remove from the oven.
2. Put the vegetable fat into a 1¾pt (1l) glass or pottery bowl. Cook, uncovered, on FULL POWER for 1½-2 minutes.
3. Remove from the oven and add the flour. Stir together to form a roux. Return to the microwave and cook, uncovered, on FULL POWER for 1 minute.
4. Remove from the oven and gradually blend in the warmed milk.
5. Return to the oven and cook, uncovered, until the sauce comes to the boil and thickens allowing approximately 2-3 minutes on FULL POWER. Beat at the end of every minute to ensure the sauce is smooth.
6. Season to taste, stir well and use as desired.

Variations

Pouring Sauce. Halve the quantity of flour and make as above.

Mushroom Sauce. Put 4oz (125g) chopped cup mushrooms and 1 tablespoon skimmed milk into a 1pt (600ml) glass or pottery dish. Leave uncovered and cook on FULL POWER for 1 minute. Add mushrooms to the pouring sauce at the same time as the warmed milk.

Caper Sauce. Add 2 level tablespoons chopped capers to the pouring sauce with seasoning.

Tip
These recipes can be made using 85% wheatmeal flour to give a rich, nutty texture and flavour.

½pt (300ml) skimmed milk
½oz (15g) vegetable fat
½oz (15g) plain flour
½-level tsp freshly-grated nutmeg
sea salt and freshly-milled black pepper

Nutmeg Sauce

Make as for White Sauce, adding the grated nutmeg after the sauce has been made. Cook, uncovered, on FULL POWER for a further minute.

Makes ¼ pt
1 tblsp wine vinegar
1 tblsp water
1 grade 3 egg and 1 grade 3 egg yolk, beaten together
2oz (50g) low fat spread, cut into small pieces
1 tblsp lemon juice
¼ level tsp whole grain mustard
sea salt and freshly-milled black pepper to taste

Low Fat Mayonnaise without Oil

One of the most useful sauces for dieters, and as good as any richer mayonnaise.

1. Pour the vinegar into a 1pt (600ml) glass or pottery jug or bowl. Cook, uncovered, on FULL POWER for 1 to 1½ minutes or until the vinegar has reduced by half.
2. Remove from the oven and add the water.
3. Add the beaten egg and yolk and stir vigorously.
4. Return to the oven and cook, uncovered, on SIMMER until the mixture is thick enough to coat the back of a wooden spoon. Allow approximately ¾ to 1 minute, beating at the end of every 15 seconds.
5. Remove from the oven and add the low fat spread. Stir well with a wooden spoon until melted.
6. Add the lemon juice, mustard and seasoning.
7. Cover and leave until cold.

2 tblsp soy sauce

1 tblsp honey

1 tblsp wine vinegar

¼ level tsp vegetable stock extract

¼pt (150ml) cold water

Sweet and Sour Sauce

This sauce is excellent served with stir fry vegetables — very simple and quick to prepare.

1. Put all the ingredients into a ½pt (300ml) glass or pottery jug.
2. Cook on FULL POWER for 2 minutes. Stir and serve hot.

Variation

For a thicker sauce, blend 1 level teaspoon cornflour into 2 teaspoons cold water in a ½pt (300ml) bowl to make a smooth paste. Stir the hot sauce into the cornflour paste. Return to the glass or pottery jug and cook, uncovered, on FULL POWER for 1 minute. Stir and serve hot.

Makes ½pt (300ml)

3oz (75g) vegetable fat or butter

1 level tsp cornflour

¼pt (150ml) skimmed milk

2 grade 3 egg yolks

1 tblsp lemon juice

sea salt and freshly-milled black pepper

Hollandaise Sauce

A classic sauce for artichokes and asparagus which is fail-proof.

1. Put the fat or butter into a 1¾pt (1l) glass or pottery bowl. Cook, uncovered, on FULL POWER for 2 minutes. Remove from the oven.
2. Tip the cornflour into a bowl and blend in 2 tablespoons of the milk. Add remaining milk.
3. Add the cornflour mixture and egg yolks to the melted fat. Beat well with a fork.
4. Cook, uncovered, for 1¼ minutes on FULL POWER until the sauce comes to the boil and thickens. Beat after every 25 seconds to ensure the sauce is smooth.

5. Add the lemon juice and seasoning. Stir round and serve.

Makes 14fl oz (400ml)

½pt (300ml) fresh pineapple juice

½oz (15g) vegetable fat

3oz (75g) green pepper, de-seeded and chopped

3oz (75g) onion, chopped

½oz (15g) wholemeal flour

2 level tsp brown pickle

2 tsp Worcestershire sauce

1 level tsp whole grain mustard

sea salt and freshly-milled black pepper to taste

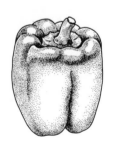

Pepper, Pickle and Pineapple Sauce

A piquant sauce designed for nut roasts and tofu dishes.

1. Pour the pineapple juice into a 1pt (600ml) glass or pottery jug. Cook, uncovered, on FULL POWER for 2 minutes. Remove from the oven.

2. Put the vegetable fat, pepper and onion into a 1¾pt (1l) bowl. Cover with cling film and puncture twice with a knife. Cook on FULL POWER for 5½ minutes to soften the vegetables. Remove from the oven.

3. Add the flour, stirring with a wooden spoon to form a roux. Return to the microwave and cook, uncovered, on FULL POWER for 1 minute.

4. Remove from the oven and, with a wooden spoon, gradually blend in the warmed pineapple juice.

5. Return to the oven and cook, uncovered, until the sauce comes to the boil and thickens. Allow approximately 4 minutes on FULL POWER. Beat at the end of every minute to ensure the sauce is smooth.

6. Add the brown pickle, Worcestershire sauce, whole grain mustard and seasoning. Stir well to mix.

7. Cook, uncovered, on FULL POWER for 2 minutes. Stir round and serve.

117

Serves 4

1oz (25g) vegetable fat

6oz (175g) onion, finely chopped

2 cloves garlic, crushed

2-4 dried red chillies, crushed

14oz (400g) can peeled tomatoes

1½ level tsp cornflour

1 bay leaf

sea salt and freshly-milled black pepper

Balkan Tomato Sauce

A hot and spicy tomato sauce which makes a distinctive accompaniment to Stuffed Aubergines and Green Pea Rissoles (pages 81 and 31). *One tip:* do not underestimate the strength of the tiny dried chillies and use only two to begin with for safety.

1. Place vegetable fat in a glass or pottery dish with the onions, garlic and chillies. Cover with a plate and cook on FULL POWER for 3 minutes.

2. Drain tomatoes and reserve juice. Chop flesh and stir into the onion mixture with a wooden spoon.

3. Blend cornflour with a little of the reserved tomato juice. Add to onion mixture with the bay leaf, seasoning and rest of reserved tomato juice.

4. Mix well with a wooden spoon. Cook, uncovered, on FULL POWER for 4 minutes, stirring every 30 seconds. Cover, leave to stand 2 to 3 minutes and use as required.

Cumberland Sauce

Makes ¾pt (450ml)

1 orange

½ lemon

4 level tblsp redcurrant jelly

1 thin slice of onion

¼pt (150ml) red wine

1 level tsp mustard powder

good pinch ground ginger

good pinch cayenne pepper

A classic and traditional unthickened red wine sauce which goes well with Stuffed Cabbage (page 84).

1. Using a potato peeler, peel thin strips of rind from half the orange and half the lemon. Cut finely into narrow, hair-line shreds. Place in a ½pt (300ml) glass or pottery jug or bowl. Add enough water to cover. Cook, uncovered, on FULL POWER for 1 minute.

2. Remove from the oven and leave to stand for 10 minutes.

3. Squeeze the juice from the whole orange and half the lemon. Pour into a small jug.

4. Put the redcurrant jelly into a 1pt (600ml) glass or pottery jug. Cook, uncovered, on FULL POWER for 1 minute. Remove from the oven and add the slice of onion. Leave to stand for 5 minutes.

5. Return to the oven and cook, uncovered, on FULL POWER for ½ minute. Remove and discard the onion.

6. Add the wine to the redcurrant jelly and stir well.

7. Combine the mustard powder, ginger, cayenne pepper, orange and lemon juice together in a small bowl. Add to the wine and redcurrant jelly. Cook, uncovered, on FULL POWER for 2-3 minutes, beating at the end of every minute to ensure the sauce is smooth.

8. Strain the shreds of peel and stir into the sauce.

Barbecue Sauce

Makes ¾pt (450ml)

2oz (50g) onion, finely chopped
3oz (75g) green pepper, de-seeded and finely chopped
1oz (25g) vegetable fat
1oz (25g) 85% wheatmeal flour
¼pt (150ml) orange juice
½pt (300ml) water
1 tblsp wine vinegar
2 tsp Worcestershire sauce
2 level tsp tomato purée
3oz (75g) cooking apple, peeled, cored and diced
1 level tblsp clear honey
1 level tsp dark raw cane sugar
sea salt and freshly-milled black pepper to taste

This is a wholesome sauce with the added health advantages of raw cane sugar and wheatmeal flour.

1. Put the onion, green pepper and vegetable fat into a 1¾pt (1l) glass or pottery bowl. Cover with cling film and puncture twice with the tip of a knife. Cook on FULL POWER for 5 minutes.
2. Remove from the oven and stir in the flour to form a roux. Cook, uncovered, on FULL POWER for 1 minute. Remove from the oven and gradually stir in the orange juice, water and wine vinegar with a wooden spoon.
3. Return to the oven and cook, uncovered, until the sauce comes to the boil and thickens, allowing approximately 4-5 minutes on FULL POWER. Beat at the end of every minute to ensure the sauce is smooth.
4. Remove from the oven and add the Worcestershire sauce, tomato purée, diced apple, clear honey, sugar and seasoning. Cook, uncovered, on FULL POWER for a further 3 minutes or until the apple is tender.
5. Serve hot with Vegetarian Kebabs (page 109).

Cider, Cheese and Apple Sauce

Makes ½pt (300ml)

6fl oz (175ml) dry cider
4fl oz (120ml) apple juice
¾oz (20g) vegetable fat
¾oz (20g) wholemeal flour
3oz (75g) Vegetarian Cheddar cheese, grated

A tangy sauce based on cider and apples which partners well with Stuffed Onions or Stuffed Tomatoes (pages 104 and 108). It is also distinguished over hard boiled eggs and with omelettes.

3oz (75g) eating apple, peeled, cored and grated

sea salt and freshly-milled black pepper to taste

1. Pour the cider and apple juice in a 1pt (600ml) glass or pottery jug. Cook, uncovered, on FULL POWER for 2 minutes. Remove from the oven.

2. Put the vegetable fat into a 1¾pt (1l) glass or pottery bowl. Cook, uncovered, on FULL POWER for 1½ minutes until melted.

3. Add flour and stir together to form a roux. Cook, uncovered, on FULL POWER for a further minute.

4. Gradually blend in the warmed cider and apple juice.

5. Cook, uncovered, for 2 to 3 minutes on FULL POWER until the sauce comes to the boil and thickens. Beat at the end of every minute to ensure the sauce is smooth.

6. Blend in the grated cheese and cook, uncovered on FULL POWER for a further ½ minute. Stir until cheese is completely melted.

7. Add apple, sea salt and freshly-milled black pepper. Cook, uncovered, on FULL POWER for 1 minute. Stir round and serve.

Strong Mustard Sauce

Makes ¾ pt

¼ pt (150ml) vegetable stock
½ pt (300ml) skimmed milk
1oz (25g) vegetable fat
1 small clove garlic, crushed
3 level tblsp 85% wheatmeal flour
½ level tsp turmeric
1 level tblsp English mustard
1 level tsp whole grain mustard
1 level tsp dark raw cane sugar
1½ tsp wine vinegar
½ tsp Worcestershire sauce
sea salt and freshly-milled black pepper to taste

A full-flavoured mustard sauce for stuffed peppers or aubergines.

1. Pour the vegetable stock and skimmed milk into a 1pt (600ml) glass or pottery jug. Cook, uncovered, on FULL POWER for 2 minutes.
2. Put the vegetable fat and garlic into a 1¾ pt (1l) glass or pottery bowl. Cook, uncovered, on FULL POWER for 3 minutes in which time the garlic should have softened.
3. Remove from oven and stir in the flour. Return to the microwave and cook, uncovered, on FULL POWER for 1 minute.
4. Gradually blend in the warmed milk and vegetable stock.
5. Cook, uncovered, for approximately 3 minutes on FULL POWER until the sauce comes to the boil and thickens. Beat at the end of every minute to ensure the sauce is smooth.
6. Remove from the oven.
7. In a small bowl, blend together the turmeric, and mustards. Add to sauce followed by sugar, vinegar, Worcestershire sauce, sea salt and freshly-milled black pepper. Stir well. Cook, uncovered, on FULL POWER for 1 minute.

Orange Sauce

Makes ¾ pt (450ml)

2 level tblsp cornflour
⅓ pt (200ml) fresh orange juice

A warmly-fragrant orange sauce, tinged with Cointreau for stuffed cabbage, stuffed jacket potatoes and lightly cooked courgettes.

8fl oz (250ml) vegetable stock

2 level tblsp redcurrant jelly

sea salt and freshly-milled black pepper

1 to 2 tblsp Cointreau (optional)

1. Blend cornflour with 4 tablespoons orange juice and leave on one side temporarily.
2. Pour rest of orange juice and vegetable stock into a 1pt (600ml) jug. Heat, uncovered, on FULL POWER for 2 minutes.
3. Gradually pour into the cornflour mixture, stirring with a wooden spoon or plastic spatula.
4. Cook, uncovered, for 2 to 3 minutes on FULL POWER until the sauce comes to the boil and thickens. Beat at the end of every minute to ensure sauce is smooth.
5. Add the redcurrant jelly and seasoning and stir well until completely smooth. Add Cointreau if liked.

Makes ½pt (300ml)

1 lemon

1 level tblsp clear marmalade jelly

½pt (300ml) water

½oz (15g) preserved ginger, chopped

1½ level tblsp cornflour

½oz (15g) dark raw cane sugar

1 tblsp Cointreau or concentrated orange squash

Marmalade and Ginger Sauce

Especially good with a sponge pudding.

1. Remove the rind from the lemon and cut it into very thin strips. Squeeze out the juice.
2. Put the marmalade jelly, water (minus 2 tablespoons), lemon rind and ginger into a 1¾pt (1l) glass or pottery bowl. Cook, uncovered, on FULL POWER for 3 minutes, stirring at the end of every minute to ensure the marmalade jelly dissolves.
3. Blend the cornflour with the 2 tablespoons of water and add to bowl of sauce.
4. Mix in sugar and lemon juice. Add the Cointreau or squash. Cook, uncovered, on FULL POWER for 2 minutes until the sauce thickens, beating at the end of every minute to ensure sauce is smooth. Remove from the oven. Stir round and serve.

123

Cranberry and Orange Sauce

Serves 4

½oz (15g) vegetable fat

2oz (50g) onion, grated

grated rind and juice of 1 large orange

2 cloves garlic, crushed

2 level tblsp flour

¼pt (150ml) water

4 level tblsp cranberry sauce

sea salt and freshly-milled black pepper to taste

An attractively-coloured and well-flavoured sauce for the Mushroom and Nut Meat Pudding (page 44).

1. Place vegetable fat, onion, orange rind and garlic into a 2pt (1.2l) glass or pottery bowl. Cover with cling film and puncture twice with the tip of a knife.
2. Cook on FULL POWER for 2 minutes.
3. Sprinkle flour on to onion mixture and stir well. Gradually blend in the orange juice, water, cranberry sauce and seasoning.
4. Cook, uncovered, on FULL POWER for 4 minutes, stirring well after each minute.

Egg Custard Sauce

Makes 1¼pt (750ml)

½oz (15g) cornflour

3 tblsp caster sugar

1pt (600ml) skimmed milk

2 grade 3 egg yolks

2 drops vanilla essence

An old friend, delicious over baked apples, stewed fruit and steamed puddings. The cornflour acts as a stabiliser and prevents curdling.

1. Mix the cornflour, sugar and 2 tablespoons of the milk together in a 2pt (1.2l) glass or pottery bowl.
2. Beat in the egg yolks with a fork.
3. Pour the remaining milk into a 2pt (1.2l) glass or pottery jug. Cook, uncovered, on FULL POWER for 5 minutes until almost boiling.
4. Gradually beat the hot milk into the egg mixture.
5. Cook for approximately 4 minutes on FULL POWER until the sauce comes to the boil and

124

thickens. Beat at the end of every minute to ensure sauce is smooth.

6. Remove from the oven and add the vanilla essence.

7. Serve hot or cold.

Makes ¾pt (450ml)

1 level tblsp cornflour

½pt (300ml) cider

4oz (125g) fresh pineapple, chopped

1oz (25g) seedless raisins

Pineapple and Cider Sauce

An exotic-tasting fruity sauce for vegetables such as aubergine, tomatoes or okra.

1. Blend the cornflour with 2 tablespoons of the cider in a small bowl.

2. Pour the remaining cider into a 1¾pt (1l) glass or pottery bowl. Cook, uncovered, on FULL POWER for 2 minutes.

3. Add the blended cornflour, stirring continually.

4. Cook, uncovered, for approximately 2 to 3 minutes on FULL POWER until the sauce comes to the boil and thickens. Beat at the end of every minute to ensure sauce is smooth.

5. Stir in pineapple and raisins. Cook, uncovered, on FULL POWER for a further minute. Stir round and serve.

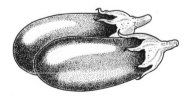

Puréed Fruits

Fruits cook in their own juice in the microwave and make excellent purées for ice creams, soufflés or mousses. Cook the fruits then allow them to cool. Remove pips or seeds then purée in a food processor or blender. Alternatively, rub mixture through a fine mesh sieve.

Apples
Core apples. Prick the skin in three or flour places with a fork. Put the apple in a glass dish and cover with cling film. Puncture twice with the tip of a knife. Cook on FULL POWER for 2½ minutes. Leave covered for 3 minutes then take off cling film. Carefully lift off the skin and spoon apple pulp into a bowl. For two apples increase cooking time to 5 minutes and standing time to 4 minutes.

Gooseberries (1lb/450g)
Cook, covered, on FULL POWER for 3 minutes.

Raspberries (1lb/450g)
or loganberries, blackberries. Cook, covered, on FULL POWER for 2½ minutes.

Rhubarb (1lb/450g)
Cut into 2in (5cm) chunks. Cook, covered, on FULL POWER for 6 minutes, stirring once during cooking.

Strawberries (1lb/450g)
Cook, uncovered, on FULL POWER for 2½ minutes.

BREADS AND CAKES

A gallery of ideas, all mouth-watering, which cook happily and successfully in the microwave. Among them are Rye Bread with Herbs, Cheese Caraway Bread, Cider Horseshoe Plait, Hot Cross Buns, Parsnip Cake, Christmas Cake and Scots Black Bun, Gingerbread, Scones, a honeyed Carob Cake, Brandy Snaps, and Fig Loaf. Bright, wholesome ideas to make baking days happy and relaxing occasions.

Makes 12 slices

---

1 level tsp dark raw cane
sugar

½pt (300ml) water

1oz (25g) fresh yeast

1lb (450g) strong 81%
wheatmeal flour

3oz (75g) Sultana Bran

---

pinch of salt

¾oz (20g) vegetable fat

½ grade 3 egg, beaten

½oz (15g) flaked almonds,
lightly toasted

*Wheatmeal Loaf
(Photo: British Alcan)*

Wheatmeal Loaf

A traditionally-shaped loaf which is sweet. A good
tea-time treat, especially nourishing for children.

1. Put the sugar and ¼pt (150ml) of the water
    into a ½pt (300ml) glass or pottery jug. Cook,
    uncovered, on FULL POWER for 45 seconds.

2. Remove from the oven and stir in the fresh
    yeast. Leave to stand for approximately 10
    minutes until the yeast forms a froth on the
    surface.

3. Put the flour, Sultana Bran and salt into a 2pt
    (1l) glass or pottery mixing bowl. Cook,
    uncovered, on FULL POWER for 30 seconds.
    Remove from the oven and rub in the
    vegetable fat.

4. Add the yeast mixture and the remaining ¼pt
    (150ml) water and mix with a wooden spoon
    to form a dough. Turn out on to a floured
    surface and knead dough for about 10 minutes
    or until it becomes smooth and elastic.

5. Return to a 4pt (2.25l) glass or pottery bowl
    that has been dampened and floured. Cover
    with a piece of floured cling film and
    puncture twice with the tip of a knife.

6. Cook on DEFROST for 45 seconds; rest for 5
    minutes. Repeat this process 3 more times until
    the dough has doubled in size.

7. Remove from the oven and re-knead the
    dough for about 5 minutes on a floured
    surface.

8. Put into a dampened and floured 2lb (1kg)
    glass or pottery loaf dish.

9. Brush with a little beaten egg and sprinkle with
    a few flaked almonds. Cover loosely with
    floured cling film and leave to stand for about
    20 minutes or until the dough has doubled in
    size and risen to the top of the dish.

10. Remove cling film and cook on FULL POWER for 4 minutes. Leave to stand 5 minutes then turn out and cool on a wire rack. Cut when cold.

Rye Bread with Herbs

A nutritious loaf with the taste of fresh herbs.

Makes 8 slices

¼pt (150ml) water

½ level tsp caster sugar

¾oz (20g) fresh yeast

4oz (125g) rye flour

4oz (125g) strong plain white flour

¼ level tsp sea salt

1oz (25g) vegetable fat

1 level tblsp chopped parsley

1 level tblsp scissor-snipped chives

1. Pour water into a ½pt (300ml) glass or pottery jug and cook, uncovered, on FULL POWER for 30 seconds.

2. Remove from oven and stir in sugar and yeast. Leave to stand for about 5 to 10 minutes or until the yeast forms a froth on the surface.

3. Put the flours and salt into a 2pt (1.2l) glass or pottery mixing bowl. Rub in fat and stir in herbs.

4. Cook, uncovered, on DEFROST for 1 minute.

5. Make a well in the centre of the flour and pour in yeast liquid. Mix well to form a dough. Turn out on to a floured surface and knead for 5 minutes.

6. Place the dough into a greased 1lb (450g) glass or pottery loaf dish and cover with floured cling film. Puncture twice with the tip of a knife. Cook on DEFROST for 45 seconds. Rest for 5 minutes. Repeat this process 3 more times until the dough has doubled in size. Remove cling film.

7. Cook, uncovered, on SIMMER for 6 minutes. Leave to stand for 3 minutes then turn out on to a cooling rack. Leave to cool.

Above: Brown Bread and Butter Pudding (p 162)
Below: Date Tea Bread (p 139)
(Photos: California Raisin Advisory Board)

Cheese Caraway Bread

Makes 10 slices

¼pt (150ml) skimmed milk

½ level tsp dark raw cane sugar

½oz (15g) fresh yeast

10oz (275g) plain unbleached flour

pinch of salt

1 grade 3 egg

4oz (125g) Vegetarian Cheddar cheese, grated

1½ level tsp caraway seeds

½ grade 3 egg, beaten (for glaze)

about 20 extra caraway seeds for sprinkling over top of loaf

A fine, savoury loaf which is good for lunch or supper with salad

1. Put the milk and sugar into a 1pt (600ml) glass or pottery jug and cook, uncovered, on FULL POWER for 30 seconds.
2. Remove from the oven and stir in the yeast. Leave to stand for 5 to 10 minutes or until the yeast forms a froth on the surface.
3. Put the flour and salt into a 2pt (1.2l) mixing bowl and cook, uncovered, on FULL POWER for 15 seconds. Remove from the oven.
4. Make a well in the centre of the flour and pour in the yeast mixture, flicking the flour over the surface to cover the yeast.
5. Cook on DEFROST for 45 seconds; rest for 5 minutes. Cook again on DEFROST for 45 seconds and rest for another 5 minutes.
6. Remove from the oven and add the egg, beating the dough well with a wooden spoon.
7. Add the grated cheese and the caraway seeds and mix to form a dough. Cover with floured cling film and puncture twice with the tip of a knife.
8. Cook on DEFROST for 35 seconds and rest for 5 minutes. Repeat this process 3 more times then remove from the oven.
9. Re-knead the dough for about 5 minutes on a floured surface.
10. Put into a dampened and floured 1lb (450g) glass loaf dish and cover loosely with floured cling film. Leave to stand for about 20 minutes until the dough has doubled in size and risen to the top of the dish.

11. Remove the cling film and brush the loaf with the beaten egg. Sprinkle on about 20 caraway seeds.

12. Cook, uncovered, on FULL POWER for 3 minutes. Remove from the oven and rest for 5 minutes. Turn out on to a cooling rack and leave to cool before slicing.

Horseshoe Plait

Makes 12 slices

½pt (300ml) apple juice

½oz (15g) fresh yeast

1lb (450g) strong wholemeal flour

pinch of salt

2oz (50g) vegetable fat

½ grade 3 egg, beaten

1 level tsp poppy seeds

This is an interestingly-shaped bread cooked on a pizza tray.

1. Pour the apple juice into a 1 pt (600ml) glass or pottery jug. Cook, uncovered, on FULL POWER for 45 seconds. Remove from oven.

2. Put the yeast and 2 tablespoons of the warmed apple juice into a small bowl. Stir well to mix. Add this yeast mixture to the remaining warmed cider. Leave to stand for about 5 to 10 minutes until the yeast forms a froth on the surface.

3. Put the flour and salt into a 4pt (2.25l) glass or pottery mixing bowl. Cook, uncovered, on FULL POWER for 30 seconds. Remove from the oven and rub in the vegetable fat.

4. Add the yeast liquid and mix to form a dough. Turn out on to a floured surface and knead for 10 minutes until smooth and elastic.

5. Place the dough into a 4pt (2.25l) floured glass or pottery bowl and cover with floured cling film. Puncture twice with the tip of a knife. Cook on DEFROST for 45 seconds; rest for 5 minutes. Repeat this process 3 more times until the dough has doubled in size.

6. Re-knead for about 5 minutes on a floured surface.

7. Divide dough into 3 equal pieces. Shape into strands of about 16in (40.5cm) in length. Plait together and shape into a horseshoe.

8. Place the plait on to a floured glass or pottery pizza tray. Cover with floured cling film. Leave to stand for about 20 minutes, until the dough has doubled in size.

9. Remove the cling film, brush the plait with beaten egg and sprinkle with poppy seeds. Cook, uncovered, on FULL POWER for 5 minutes.

10. Remove from the oven and rest for 5 minutes. Turn out on to a cooling rack and leave to cool.

Serves about 12

6oz (175g) sunflower margarine
6oz (175g) soft dark brown sugar
4oz (125g) wholewheat flour
4oz (125g) 81% self raising wheatmeal flour
1 level tsp mixed spice
½ level tsp freshly-grated nutmeg
3 grade 3 eggs, at room temperature, beaten
2 level tblsp black treacle
pinch of bicarbonate of soda
2 tblsp brandy
8oz (225g) seeded raisins
8oz (225g) currants
8oz (225g) sultanas
2oz (50g) natural colour glacé cherries, finely chopped
2oz (50g) cut mixed peel
2oz (50g) blanched almonds, finely chopped

Christmas Cake

You can cook this large, rich fruit cake in less than three-quarters of an hour in the microwave.

1. Line a 4pt (2.25l) glass or pottery soufflé dish with cling film.
2. Cream together the margarine and sugar until light and fluffy.
3. Mix together the flours, mixed spice and grated nutmeg.
4. In a small glass bowl, beat the eggs with treacle, bicarbonate of soda and brandy.
5. Gradually beat the eggs etc into the creamed mixture, adding a little flour if the mixture begins to curdle.
6. Stir in remaining flour, fruit, cherries, peel and nuts. Mix well.
7. Spoon the fruit cake mixture into the cake dish. Smooth the surface, making a slight well in the centre.
8. Cook on DEFROST for 42 minutes. Leave to stand for 30 minutes before turning out on to a cooling rack.
9. Decorate with almond paste and icing as required.

Carrot Cake

Serves 8

6oz (175g) brown self-raising flour

6oz (175g) soft margarine

6oz (175g) light soft brown sugar

3 grade 3 eggs, at room temperature

1 level tsp cinnamon

6oz (175g) carrots, finely grated

grated rind of 1 lemon

1 tblsp lemon juice

Icing

8oz (225g) cream or curd cheese

2oz (50g) icing sugar

4 tsp lemon juice

For decoration

mimosa balls

angelica leaves

1. Place flour, margarine, sugar, eggs and cinnamon in a mixing bowl. Beat well until ingredients are thoroughly combined.
2. Fold in grated carrot, lemon rind and juice.
3. Spoon into a 2pt (1.2l) savarin mould lined with clingfilm. Level surface.
4. Cook, uncovered, on FULL POWER for 10 minutes if mould is plastic, 8 minutes if mould is glass.
5. Leave in container to stand for 5 minutes before turning out on to a wire rack to cool.
6. Beat together cheese, icing sugar and lemon juice until smooth. Spread over cake to cover.
7 Decorate with mimosa balls and angelica leaves.

Parsnip Cake

Makes 8 slices

6oz (175g) vegetable fat, softened

6oz (175g) demerara sugar

3 grade 4 eggs, at room temperature, beaten

Do use freshly grated nutmeg when making this moist cake — the fragrant smell is one of the pleasures of cooking. The cake keeps well in an airtight container.

1. Line a 7in (18cm) deep glass or pottery cake dish with cling film.

8oz (225g) self raising
wholemeal flour

12oz (350g) parsnip, peeled
and grated

½ level tsp freshly grated
nutmeg

pinch of sea salt

1 tblsp lemon juice

2. Cream fat and sugar together. Gradually beat in eggs, then fold in flour, grated parsnip, nutmeg and salt. Mix well to a soft dropping consistency with the lemon juice.
3. Spoon the mixture into the cake dish.
4. Cook on SIMMER for 12 minutes. Stand for 8 minutes.
5. Turn out on to a cooling rack covered with a layer of cling film. Cool completely.

Serves 8

4oz (125g) sunflower
margarine, at room
temperature

4oz (125g) light, soft raw
cane sugar

2 grade 3 eggs, at room
temperature, beaten

2 tblsp concentrated
apple juice

4oz (125g) 81% wheatmeal
self raising flour

3oz (75g) dessert apple

Apple Ring

A deliciously moist cake.

1. Line a 9in (23cm) glass ring mould with cling film.
2. Put margarine and sugar into a mixing bowl and cream together until light and fluffy. Beat in the eggs, one at a time, then fold in the flour. Lastly stir in the apple juice.
3. Spread half the cake mixture into the lined ring mould.
4. Peel the apple then coarsely grate on to kitchen paper. Discard the core. Cover the grated apple with another piece of kitchen paper and press gently to remove any excess moisture.
5. Sprinkle grated apple over the cake mixture in the ring mould, then spread the remaining mixture over the apple.
6. Cook, uncovered, on FULL POWER for 5 minutes. Rest for 15 minutes. Turn out on to a cooling rack and peel off the cling film.

Gingerbread

Makes 16 portions

5oz (150g) soya margarine

4oz (125g) soft brown sugar

4oz (125g) ginger jam or
orange marmalade

2oz (50g) clear honey

7oz (200g) self raising
wholemeal flour

1 level tsp ground ginger

½ level tsp mixed spice

2 grade 3 eggs, at room
temperature, beaten

This gingerbread is made by the 'melting method'
which is particularly good in a microwave. It takes
only half the time to cook compared with a
conventional oven and is a light, honey-coloured
golden brown. Quite delicious!

1. Put margarine, sugar, ginger jam and honey in a
   3½pt (2l) mixing bowl. Cook, uncovered, on
   REHEAT for 2 minutes.
2. Stir with a wooden spoon until the mixture is
   well-blended and smooth.
3. Cool for 10 minutes.
4. Meanwhile, line an 11in × 8in (28cm × 20cm)
   shallow glass or pottery dish with cling film.
5. Tip flour into a bowl. Sift in spices. Add to the
   melted fat mixture with the beaten eggs. Beat
   well until smooth.
6. Pour into the lined shallow dish and cook,
   uncovered, on SIMMER for 14 minutes. Remove
   from microwave and allow gingerbread to cool in
   dish. Invert on to a wire rack, peel away cling film
   then turn the right way up. Leave until
   completely cool before cutting.

Tip
The cake improves on keeping.

Buttermilk Scones

Makes 8-10

½ level tsp bicarbonate of
soda

pinch of sea salt

8oz (225g) self raising
wholemeal flour

Scones are simple to prepare and delicious to eat,
whether hot or cold and the variations to the
basic recipe are endless. For example, one can use
natural yogurt or sour milk instead of buttermilk
or add herbs, cheese, spices, grated lemon rind,
sultanas, etc, to the flour before adding the liquid.

2oz (50g) vegetable fat

scant ¼pt (150ml) orange-flavoured buttermilk

1. Stir bicarbonate of soda and salt into flour. Rub in fat and mix to a soft dough with the buttermilk. Knead lightly on a floured board.
2. Roll out dough and stamp out 8 to 10 rounds with a 2½in (6cm) cutter. Place on a large, lightly greased glass or pottery plate.
3. Cook, uncovered, on FULL POWER for 4 minutes. Leave to rest for 5 minutes.
4. Serve warm or cold.

Makes 8-10

3 large spring onions, very finely chopped

2oz (50g) vegetable fat

½ level tsp bicarbonate of soda

pinch of sea salt

8oz (225g) malted wheatmeal flour

scant ¼pt (150ml) milk

Granary and Spring Onion Scones

1. Place spring onions and ½oz (15g) fat into a glass or pottery mixing bowl. Cover with cling film and puncture twice with the tip of a knife.
2. Cook on FULL POWER for 2 minutes.
3. Stir bicarbonate of soda and salt into flour. Rub in remaining fat. Stir in spring onions and mix to a soft dough with milk. Knead lightly on a floured board.
4. Follow above recipe from stage 2.

Brandy Snaps

Makes about 12

2oz (50g) sunflower margarine

2oz (50g) golden syrup

1¾oz (40g) golden granulated raw cane sugar

1¾oz (40g) malted wheatmeal flour

1 level tsp ground ginger

These cook like magic in the microwave without the hassle of sticking.

1. Put margarine into a 2pt (1.2l) glass or pottery bowl. Cook, uncovered, on SIMMER for 1¼ minutes.
2. Add golden syrup and sugar. Stir with a wooden spoon. Cook, uncovered, on FULL POWER for 1 minute.
3. Mix together the flour and ground ginger and stir into the syrup mixture.
4. Put 4 teaspoons of the mixture, well apart, on a glass pizza plate or large flat glass plate. Alternatively, put one tablespoon of the mixture in the centre of a glass plate.
5. Cook on FULL POWER for 1½ minutes. Cool for 5 minutes, then carefully lift off plate. Roll round a wooden spoon handle. Transfer to a cooling rack. Fill with whipped cream when cold.

Fruit Loaf

Makes 8 slices

6oz (175g) mixed dried fruit

½pt (300ml) apple juice

5oz (150g) 81% wheatmeal flour

1½oz (40g) walnuts, chopped

3oz (75g) soft raw cane sugar

1 grade 3 egg, at room temperature, beaten

Ideal for picnics, this fruit loaf keeps well and can be served with or without low fat spread.

1. Put dried fruit and apple juice into a 3pt (1.75l) glass or pottery bowl. Cover with cling film and puncture twice with the tip of a knife. Cook on FULL POWER for 5 minutes, remove from oven and allow to stand for 5 minutes.
2. Mix flour, walnuts and sugar together. Stir into the fruit mixture. Add the beaten egg and mix well.

3. Line a 1lb (450g) glass or pottery loaf dish with cling film. Add the cake mixture and cook, uncovered, on SIMMER for 8 minutes.

4. Allow to stand for 5 minutes then turn out and cool on a wire rack.

Date Tea Bread

Makes 8 slices

4oz (125g) fresh dates, stoned and chopped

4oz (125g) raisins

4oz (125g) soft dark raw cane sugar

1fl oz (25ml) cold brewed tea

4oz (125g) 81% self raising wheatmeal flour

½ level tsp mixed spice

1 grade 3 egg, at room temperature, beaten

10 whole blanched almonds

To glaze

2 level tblsp honey

A healthy fruited tea loaf, lightly spiced and topped with almonds.

1. Line a 1lb (450g) glass or pottery loaf dish with cling film.

2. Put fruit, sugar and tea into a 3pt (1.75l) glass or pottery bowl. Cover with cling film and puncture twice with the tip of a knife. Cook on FULL POWER for 5 minutes.

3. Remove from the oven and stir in the flour, spice and egg. Mix well to form a thick batter.

4. Spread smoothly into the loaf dish and arrange the almonds in a pattern on top.

5. Cook, uncovered, on SIMMER for 8 minutes. Allow to stand in loaf dish for 5 minutes.

6. Put the honey in a ½pt (300ml) glass or pottery bowl. Cook, uncovered, on WARM for 3 minutes.

7. Turn the date tea bread out of the loaf dish on to a wire cooling rack. Carefully peel off the cling film and brush the top with the warmed honey.

8. Leave until cold before slicing and spreading with margarine or butter.

Simnel Cake

Makes 12 slices

4oz (125g) sunflower margarine
4oz (125g) light brown soft sugar
3oz (75g) wholewheat flour
3oz (75g) 81% self raising wheatmeal flour
½ level tsp mixed spice
pinch ground cinnamon
2 grade 3 eggs, at room temperature, beaten
1 level tsp black treacle
pinch bicarbonate of soda
2½ tblsp sweet sherry
1lb (450g) mixed dried fruit
1oz (25g) cut mixed peel
Almond paste
4oz (125g) ground almonds
2oz (50g) caster sugar
2oz (50g) icing sugar, sifted
4 drops almond essence
1 grade 4 egg, beaten
2 level tsp icing sugar

This cake was traditionally served on Mothering Sunday but is now more generally made for Easter.

1. Line a 7in (18cm) deep glass cake dish with cling film.
2. Cream margarine with sugar until light and fluffy.
3. Tip flours into a bowl and sift in spices.
4. Beat the eggs, treacle, bicarbonate of soda and sherry in a small glass bowl.
5. Gradually beat the eggs etc into the creamed mixture, adding a little flour if the mixture begins to curdle.
6. Stir in the flour, fruit and peel.
7. Sieve together ground almonds and sugars. Add the almond essence and the egg. Knead lightly together to make a smooth ball. Roll out on a board lightly sprinkled with icing sugar to a circle 6in (15cm) diameter.
8. Spoon half the fruit cake mixture into the cake dish.
9. Lay the almond paste on top.
10. Spoon the remaining fruit mixture over the almond paste. Smooth over the surface, making a slight 'well' in the centre.
11. Cook, uncovered, on DEFROST for 30 minutes. Leave to stand for 20 minutes before turning out on to a cooling rack.

Tip
If you want to decorate it traditionally, make up another quantity of almond paste and use three-quarters of it to cover the top of the cake. Use the remainder to make little Easter eggs (toast them lightly, using the conventional grill). Arrange a nest of eggs in the centre of the cake. Fill with sifted icing sugar or white glacé icing.

Scottish Black Bun

Makes 10-12 slices

Pastry

8oz (225g) 100% wholewheat plain flour

4oz (125g) vegetable fat

4 tblsp cold water

1 grade 3 egg, beaten

Filling

8oz (225g) seeded raisins

4oz (125g) sultanas

4oz (125g) currants

1oz (25g) cut mixed peel

2oz (50g) blanched almonds, finely chopped

4oz (125g) 100% wholewheat plain flour

½ level tsp ground cinnamon

¼ level tsp ground ginger

¼ level tsp ground nutmeg

¼ level tsp mixed spice

½ level tsp cream of tartar

½ level tsp bicarbonate of soda

2oz (50g) soft dark brown sugar

1 grade 3 egg, at room temperature, beaten

4 tblsp whisky

2 tblsp skimmed milk, at room temperature

This recipe should be made several days before it is eaten to allow time for the cake to mature. The cake itself is fatless.

1. Lightly grease the sides and line the base of an 8in (20cm) deep-sided flan dish with non-stick cooking parchment paper. (Use a dish 2in or 5cm deep.)

2. To make pastry, tip flour into a bowl. Add fat and rub into flour until it resembles fine breadcrumbs. Mix to a firm dough with water.

3. Roll out three-quarters of the pastry and use to line the flan dish. Prick well all over, especially where the sides meet the base. Rest flan for ½ hour in the refrigerator. Wrap remaining pastry in cling film and leave in refrigerator.

4. Line flan with kitchen paper and cook, uncovered, on FULL POWER for 6 minutes.

5. Remove from oven and take out kitchen paper. Brush with the beaten egg to seal the holes. Return to the microwave and cook on FULL POWER for a further minute. Leave to cool.

6. Mix together all the filling ingredients and spoon into the cooked flan.

7. Roll out the remaining pastry into a circle 8in (20cm) diameter and use to cover the fruit. Seal edges well. Brush pastry with remaining beaten egg and prick all over with a fork.

8. Cook, uncovered, on DEFROST for 20 minutes.

9. Cool in the dish then gently ease the sides with a spatula and turn out on to a cooling rack.

10. Store in an airtight tin when completely cool.

141

Banana Bread

Makes 8 slices

3 large ripe bananas

6oz (175g) soya margarine, at room temperature

6oz (175g) soft dark brown sugar

2 level tsp baking powder

½ level tsp cinnamon

¼ level tsp sea salt

8oz (225g) malted wheatmeal flour

1 grade 1 egg, beaten

5 walnuts, chopped

4oz (125g) sultanas

A lovely, moist cake which should be kept for two to three days before eating.

1. Line a 2lb (1kg) glass loaf dish with cling film.
2. Peel the bananas into a 4pt (2.25l) bowl and mash finely with a fork.
3. Beat in the margarine then mix in sugar.
4. Sieve together baking powder, cinnamon and salt. Add flour. Fold into banana mixture with beaten egg, walnuts and sultanas.
5. Spread the mixture evenly into the prepared dish.
6. Cook, uncovered, on FULL POWER for 11 minutes. Remove from oven and rest for 10 minutes.
7. Lift the cake out of the dish on to a cooling rack and carefully remove the cling film.
8. Leave to cool and store airtight for a few days.

Apricot and Date Crunch Wedges

Makes 8

3oz (75g) 81% wheatmeal self raising flour

3oz (75g) oatmeal

4oz (125g) sunflower margarine

3oz (75g) dark raw cane sugar

4oz (125g) dried apricots, soaked overnight

2oz (50g) fresh dates

A delicious, energy-packed snack.

1. Put the flour, oats and margarine into a mixing bowl and rub gently with the fingertips until the mixture is crumbly.
2. Add the sugar and stir well.
3. Line a 7in (18cm) round glass or pottery soufflé dish with cling film. Spread half the mixture into the dish and press down well.

4. Drain the apricots and chop them. Chop the dates.

5. Spread the fruit mixture over the oat mixture. Sprinkle on the remaining oat mixture and press down well.

6. Cook, uncovered, on FULL POWER for 5½ minutes.

7. Remove from the oven and rest until cold. Carefully remove from dish and transfer to a plate. Gently lift the cling film away from the base. Cut into wedges before serving.

8. Store leftovers in an airtight container.

Nutty Apricot Cake

Makes 8 slices

1oz (25g) dark raw cane sugar

1 oz (25g) soya margarine

2oz (50g) cob or hazelnuts, coarsely chopped

8oz (225g) fresh apricots, halved and stones removed

4oz (125g) soya margarine

4oz (125g) dark raw cane sugar

2 grade 3 eggs, at room temperature

4oz (125g) 85% wheatmeal self raising flour

1oz (25g) cob or hazelnuts, finely chopped

1 tblsp skimmed milk, at room temperature

An attractive-to-look-at and fine-flavoured upside down cake.

1. Line an 8in (20cm) glass or pottery cake dish with cling film.

2. Cream together 1oz (25g) sugar and 1oz (25g) soya margarine. Spread over base of cake dish.

3. Arrange chopped nuts and apricot halves (cut sides down) over the bottom of the cake dish.

4. Put all the remaining ingredients into a 4pt (2.25l) mixing bowl and beat together well for 3 minutes by hand or for 1½ minutes with an electric mixer.

5. Transfer the mixture to the cake dish and spread evenly over the nuts and apricots.

6. Cook on FULL POWER for 6 minutes. Rest for 10 minutes then turn the cake out on to a cooling rack. Allow to cool completely before cutting.

143

Hot Cross Buns

Makes 12

¼pt (150ml) skimmed milk

2fl oz (50ml) water

1lb (450g) plain unbleached flour

1 level tsp light raw cane sugar

1oz (25g) fresh yeast

½ level tsp salt

1½ level tsp mixed spice

2oz (50g) light raw cane sugar

2oz (50g) soya margarine, at room temperature

1 grade 3 egg, beaten

2oz (50g) currants

2oz (50g) mixed peel, chopped

½ grade 3 egg, beaten

1oz (25g) flaked almonds

2 level tblsp clear honey

Glowing, almond-topped Hot Cross Buns which take minutes to cook in the microwave.

1. Put the milk and water into a 1pt (600ml) glass or pottery jug. Cook, uncovered, on FULL POWER for 45 seconds. Remove from oven.

2. Sieve 4oz (125g) of the flour into a 1¾pt (1l) glass or pottery bowl. Add the 1 teaspoon of sugar and crumble in the yeast with fingers.

3. Stir in the warmed milk and water. Leave the mixture until a froth forms on the surface.

4. Sift the remaining flour with the salt and spice. Add the remaining 2oz (50g) sugar.

5. Stir the soya margarine and egg into the risen yeast mixture. Add to flour, followed by the currants and mixed peel. Stir well to form a dough.

6. Turn out on to a floured surface and knead dough for about 10 minutes until smooth and elastic.

7. Divide the dough in half. Sub-divide one-half into 6 pieces and shape into buns. Leave remaining dough in a bowl, covered with cling film. Put the 6 buns on to a floured 10in (25cm) glass or pottery dish. Cover with floured cling film and puncture twice with the tip of a knife.

8. Cook on DEFROST for 45 seconds. Rest for 5 minutes. Repeat this process 3 more times. Remove from the oven.

9. Remove the cling film and cut crosses into the buns. Brush the beaten egg and sprinkle the cross with flaked almonds. Cook on FULL POWER for 3½ minutes.

Orange and Blackberry Lattice Flan (p 151)
(Photo: Corning)

144

10. Remove from the oven and rest for 5 minutes before turning out on to a cooling rack.

11. Brush with honey and leave to cool.

12. Repeat the last 4 steps with the remaining dough.

Honey and Carob Cake

Makes 6-8 slices

4oz (125g) vegetable fat, at kitchen temperature

4oz (125g) soft brown sugar

2 grade 4 eggs, beaten

4oz (125g) self raising wholemeal flour

1oz (25g) carob powder

2 level tblsp honey

Fudge icing

½oz (15g) vegetable fat

2 tblsp milk

1 level tblsp carob powder

5oz (150g) icing sugar, sieved

A very light-textured and tender cake with a toothsome icing. A tea-time special.

1. Line a 7in (18cm) deep glass cake dish smoothly with cling film.

2. Cream fat and sugar together. Gradually beat in eggs, and fold in flour and carob powder. Stir in honey and mix well.

3. Spoon mixture into the prepared dish and spread level.

4. Cook, uncovered, on SIMMER for 7 minutes. Allow to stand for 5 minutes.

5. Lift sponge out of dish on to a cooling rack lined with cling film. Cool completely. Remove film lining with care as cake is delicate.

6. To make icing, place fat, milk and carob powder into a glass or pottery mixing bowl.

7. Cook, uncovered, on FULL POWER for 1½ minutes.

8. Beat in icing sugar until smooth and fairly thick.

9. Spread over top of cake with a rounded knife.

Carrot Cake (p 134)
(Photo: Flour Advisory Bureau)

Makes 8 slices

4oz (125g) soya margarine

6oz (175g) soft brown sugar

4oz (125g) 85% wheatmeal
self raising flour

4oz (125g) 81% wheatmeal
flour

pinch of salt

2 grade 3 eggs, at room
temperature

2 tblsp skimmed milk, at
room temperature

1 tblsp fresh lemon juice

grated rind of 1 lemon

Wheatmeal Madeira Cake

A golden oldie, enriched with fibre.

1. Line a 7in (18cm) glass or pottery soufflé dish with cling film.
2. Put all the ingredients into a 4pt (2.25l) mixing bowl. Beat well together for about 3 minutes by hand or 1½ minutes with an electric mixer.
3. Spread smoothly into lined dish
4. Cook, uncovered, on FULL POWER for 5½ minutes.
5. Rest for 5 minutes then lift the cake out of the dish. Transfer to a cooling rack. Carefully lift off the cling film then cut into wedges when cold.

Makes 8 slices

4oz (125g) All-Bran

2oz (50g) dark raw cane
sugar

6oz (175g) fresh green figs,
washed and chopped

4 level tsp set honey

½pt (300ml) skimmed milk

5oz (150g) 81% wheatmeal
self raising flour

Fig Loaf

An exotic health cake made with fresh green figs.

1. Put All-Bran, sugar, figs, honey and milk into a 3pt (1.75l) glass or pottery bowl. Cover with cling film and puncture twice with the tip of a knife. Cook on WARM for 5 minutes.
2. Remove from oven, uncover and mix in flour.
3. Line a 1lb (450g) glass or pottery loaf dish with cling film. Add bran and fig mixture. Cook, uncovered, on ROAST for 9 minutes, stand for 1 minute and then cook on SIMMER for 2 minutes.
4. Allow to stand in dish for 5 minutes and then turn out on to a cooling rack and carefully remove the cling film.

5. Allow to cool completely before serving sliced with margarine or honey.

Tip
If fresh figs are not available, substitute 4oz (125g) dried figs.

Orange Bran Cake

Serves 8

4oz (125g) vegetable fat

4oz (125g) soft dark raw cane sugar

grated rind and juice of 1 orange

6oz (175g) 81% wheatmeal self raising flour

2oz (50g) All-Bran

2 grade 3 eggs, at room temperature, beaten

Filling

2 tblsp orange marmalade (see page 170)

Icing

4oz (125g) icing sugar

1 tblsp fresh orange juice

To decorate

3 slices of fresh orange

A tangy, orange cake for any occasion.

1. Put the vegetable fat, sugar, grated rind and juice of the orange into a 3pt (1.75l) glass or pottery bowl. Cook, uncovered, on ROAST for 2½ minutes.

2. Remove from the oven, stir to dissolve sugar then cook on ROAST for a further 2½ minutes until the fat is melted.

3. Add the flour, All-Bran and the beaten egg. Mix well.

4. Line an 8in (20cm) deep glass or pottery cake dish with cling film. Add cake mixture and spread top evenly.

5. Cook, uncovered, on FULL POWER for 5 minutes. Remove from the oven and allow to stand in the dish for 5 minutes.

6. Turn the cake on to a wire cooling rack and carefully remove the cling film. Allow to cool completely then cut in half horizontally. Spread one half with the orange marmalade and sandwich cakes together.

7. To make the icing, mix orange juice and icing sugar to a smooth paste. Spread evenly over top of cake.

8. Leave until icing has set then decorate with fresh orange slices.

Chocolate Truffles

64 Truffles

5oz (150g) dark bitter chocolate

2oz (50g) vegetable fat

2 tblsp rum

1 grade 3 egg, beaten

4oz (125g) cake crumbs (leftovers from sponge cake or upside down pudding)

12oz (350g) icing sugar, sieved

3 level tblsp cocoa powder

This recipe is sheer self indulgence, but it is a useful way of using up stale cake crumbs. If you make a batch and freeze them, you can quickly thaw the truffles in the microwave and hand them round to unexpected guests. They are also good for Christmas presents.

1. Break chocolate into a 3pt (1.75l) glass or pottery bowl. Add vegetable fat and cook on FULL POWER for 3 minutes. Stir well with a wooden spoon to blend.
2. Stir the rum into the chocolate mixture with the beaten egg and mix well.
3. Gradually work in the cake crumbs and icing sugar.
4. Place a sheet of foil in an 8in (20cm) square cake tin. Spread truffle mixture evenly in the tin and transfer to the refrigerator to set.
5. When firm (about 1½ hours) turn cake tin upside down on to a chopping board to release the truffle mixture. Peel off the foil and reserve it for later.
6. Cut the chocolate into eight 1in (2.5cm) strips. Turn and repeat cutting in the other direction to make 64 squares.
7. Sprinkle the cocoa powder on to the foil and lightly roll each truffle square into the cocoa powder.
8. Transfer truffles to a large baking tin or glass dish and freeze until firm. Store in freezer bags.
9. To serve, thaw the truffles in batches of 12 by transferring them to a shallow, 8in (20cm) glass or pottery dish. Cook, uncovered, on DEFROST for 40 seconds.

FRUITS AND PUDDINGS

Old and new faces introduce themselves in this mouth-watering section of pudding recipes which are designed to suit every season of the year and every possible occasion. Why not try Apple and Berry Meringue Flan, Mincemeat and Apple Roly Poly, Banana and Raspberry Baked Custard, Crunchy Baked Grapefruit, Mango Flan, Rhubarb and Raisin Flan, home-made Yogurt, Maple Tart, Crème Caramels and Christmas Pudding? And many more besides for memorable dinner parties and day to day eating.

Serves 6

3oz (75g) vegetable fat
8oz (225g) muesli
4oz (125g) raw cane demerara sugar
juice of one lemon
2lbs (1kg) cooking apples
¼pt (150ml) water
1 extra tblsp water

Apple Brown Betty

A tangy autumn pudding using Bramley apples.

1. Put vegetable fat into a 3pt (1.75l) glass or pottery bowl. Melt for 2 minutes, uncovered, on FULL POWER. Stir in muesli and sugar.
2. Pour lemon juice and water into a fairly large bowl. Add peeled and cored apple slices and toss well to prevent browning. Drain.
3. Pour extra tablespoon of water into a 7in (18cm) greased glass or pottery cake dish. Arrange a layer of apples over base.
4. Fill with alternate layers of muesli mixture and apples, ending with muesli.
5. Cook, uncovered, on FULL POWER for 6 minutes. Leave to stand for 5 minutes then serve hot with cream or custard.

Serves 4

Filling
1oz (25g) desiccated coconut
3oz (75g) stoned dates, finely chopped
2oz (50g) sultanas
2oz (50g) soft brown sugar
4 x 8oz (225g) cooking apples, cored and skin pricked in 3 or 4 places

Baked Stuffed Apples

A very quick dessert to prepare and the assortment of fillings is endless. For example, why not try chopped dried apricots mixed with freshly grated nutmeg and honey; or a mixture of chopped nuts, grated orange rind, glacé cherries and chopped dried banana?

1. Mix ingredients for filling together.
2. Place apples on a large glass or pottery plate. Pack centres with filling. Cover with cling film and puncture twice with the tip of a knife.
3. Cook on FULL POWER for 6 minutes. Keep covered and leave to stand for 6 minutes before serving.

150

Serves 6

Pastry

3oz (75g) vegetable fat

6oz (175g) self raising
wholemeal flour

grated rind of 1 orange

3 tblsp cold water

Filling

8oz (225g) fresh or frozen
blackberries, thawed

3 large oranges, peeled and
flesh coarsely chopped

2oz (50g) soft brown sugar

a little freshly-grated nutmeg

1 level tblsp cornflour or 2
level tblsp if using frozen
blackberries

Orange and Blackberry Lattice Flan

A rich red flan which goes well with custard, ice cream, cream or natural yogurt.

1. To make pastry, sieve flour into bowl, add fat and rub in until it resembles fine breadcrumbs. Stir in orange rind. Add water and mix to a firm dough.

2. Roll out three-quarters of the pastry on a floured surface and use to line an 8½in (21.5cm) round shallow dish. Prick well all over, especially where the sides meet the base. Rest for ½ hour in the refrigerator.

3. Line the flan with kitchen paper and cook, uncovered, on FULL POWER for 6 minutes.

4. Remove from oven and take out kitchen paper. Brush with the beaten egg to seal the holes. Cook on FULL POWER for a further minute. Leave to cool.

5. Stir fruit, sugar and nutmeg together. Sprinkle cornflour over the top and fold in. Transfer to flan case.

6. Roll out remaining pastry, plus trimmings, into a rectangle. Cut into 10 x ½in (1.25cm) thin strips.

7. Arrange in a lattice pattern over the fruit, moistening pastry edges with a little water to seal.

8. Cook, uncovered, on FULL POWER for 5 minutes. Leave to stand for 3 minutes before serving.

151

Caribbean Bananas

Serves 4

1oz (25g) safflower margarine

1½oz (40g) muscovado dark cane sugar

pinch ground cinnamon

4 bananas

2 tblsp dark rum

2oz (50g) chopped walnuts

1. Cream together the margarine, sugar and cinnamon.
2. Peel the bananas and split each one in half horizontally. Arrange sliced bananas in a 9in (23cm) glass or pottery flan dish.
3. Dot the bananas with the sugar mixture. Cover dish with cling film and puncture twice with the tip of a knife.
4. Cook on FULL POWER for 3 minutes. Remove the cling film and sprinkle over the rum and chopped walnuts.
5. Serve immediately.

Banana and Raspberry Baked Custard

Serves 4-6

½pt (300ml) milk

8oz (225g) raspberries

2oz (50g) soft brown sugar

2 grade 4 eggs, beaten

12oz (350g) bananas, peeled and sliced

To decorate

(1oz) 25g desiccated coconut, toasted

1. Place milk, raspberries and sugar into a 2pt (1.2l) glass or pottery mixing bowl. Cover with cling film and puncture twice with the tip of a knife.
2. Cook on FULL POWER for 2 minutes.
3. Beat in eggs.
4. Place bananas over base of a 2pt (1.2l) glass or pottery dish. Pour raspberry custard over the top. Cover with cling film and puncture twice with the tip of a knife.

152

5. Cook on DEFROST for 15 minutes until just set.

6. Chill before serving with desiccated coconut sprinkled over the top.

Rhubarb and Raisin Flan

Serves 6

Pastry

4oz (125g) wheatmeal flour

½ level tsp cinnamon

½ level tsp ground ginger

2oz (50g) vegetable fat

approx 2 tblsp cold water

½ grade 4 egg, beaten

Filling

1lb (450g) rhubarb, washed and sliced

2oz (50g) raisins

juice and rind of one lemon

2 tblsp soft brown sugar

Crumble

3 level tblsp wheatmeal flour

2 level tblsp soft brown sugar

½ level tsp cinnamon

½ level tsp ground ginger

2oz (50g) shelled walnuts, chopped

A spicy rhubarb and raisin dessert with a crunchy nut topping.

1. To make pastry, tip flour into a mixing bowl then sift in cinnamon and ginger. Add fat and rub in until mixture resembles fine breadcrumbs. Mix to a firm dough with water.

2. Roll out pastry on a floured surface and use to line an 8in (20cm) flan dish. Prick well all over especially where the sides meet the base. Line with kitchen paper and cook, uncovered, on FULL POWER for 6 minutes.

3. Remove from oven and take out kitchen paper. Brush with beaten egg to seal holes. Cook on FULL POWER for a further minute. Leave to cool.

4. Place rhubarb, raisins, lemon juice, lemon rind and sugar in a glass or pottery 3½pt (2l) mixing bowl and cook on FULL POWER for 3 minutes. Leave to cool.

5. Mix together crumble ingredients.

6. Spread rhubarb in flan and sprinkle over crumble. Cook, uncovered, on FULL POWER for 3 minutes. Leave to stand for 3 minutes.

7. Serve hot or cold with a little double cream.

153

Apple and Berry Meringue Flan

Serves 6-8

Flan case

3oz (75g) vegetable fat

6oz (175g) plain wheatmeal flour

1 grade 3 egg yolk

cold water to mix

Filling

8oz (225g) cooking apples, peeled, cored and sliced

2 tblsp water

8oz (225g) raspberries

2oz (50g) soft brown sugar

¼ level tsp of ground cinnamon

1 grade 3 egg yolk

1 level tblsp cornflour

Meringue

2 grade 3 egg whites

4oz (125g) caster sugar

A sweet-sour, fruity flan, gently spiced with cinnamon and topped with delicate meringue.

1. To make pastry, sieve flour into bowl, add fat and rub in finely. Add egg yolk and enough water to form a stiffish paste.

2. Roll out on a floured surface and use to line a 9in (23cm) glass or pottery flan dish. Prick well all over, especially where the sides meet the base. Rest for ½ hour in the refrigerator.

3. Line the flan with kitchen paper and cook, uncovered, on FULL POWER for 6 minutes.

4. Remove from oven and take out kitchen paper. Brush with beaten egg to seal holes. Cook on FULL POWER for a further minute. Leave to cool.

5. Place apples and 1 tablespoon water in a 2pt (1.2l) glass or pottery mixing bowl. Cover with cling film and puncture twice with the tip of a knife.

6. Cook on FULL POWER for 2 minutes. Mash to a purée. Stir in raspberries, sugar, cinnamon and egg yolk. Blend cornflour with remaining water then stir into mixture. Spread into flan case.

7. Cook, uncovered, on ROAST for 4 minutes.

8. Beat egg whites stiffly. Add half the sugar and whisk until meringue forms stiff peaks. Fold in remaining sugar.

9. Spread over fruit, taking meringue right to pastry edge.

10. Cook on ROAST for 6 minutes. Brown quickly under grill if liked. Serve hot or cold.

Fruit Compôte

Serves 4-6

8oz (225g) gooseberries, topped and tailed

1lb (450g) plums, stoned and quartered

8oz (225g) pears, peeled, cored and sliced

8oz (225g) cooking apples, peeled, cored and sliced

honey or maple syrup

Use fruits which are in season to make this compôte all the year round. Simply substitute one fruit for another but keep to the same weight or else you will have to alter the cooking time. Always prepare the fruit which does not spoil first and leave apples, pears, etc, which go brown, until last.

1. Prepare all the fruit and mix together in a 3½pt (2l) glass or pottery bowl.
2. Cover with a plate or matching lid.
3. Cook on FULL POWER for 7 to 8 minutes until fruit is tender, stirring once during cooking. Stand for 3 minutes.
4. Sweeten to taste with honey or syrup.
5. Serve hot or cold.

Spiced Junket

Serves 4

1pt (600ml) skimmed milk

1 level tblsp clear honey

1 tsp rennet essence, from a vegetarian or health food shop

1 grade 4 egg, beaten

¼ level tsp grated nutmeg

A traditional dessert best eaten with soft fruits or compôtes (see above).

1. Pour the milk into a 3pt (1.75l) glass or pottery bowl and cook, uncovered, on FULL POWER for 2 minutes. REMEMBER do not overheat the milk.
2. Add the honey, rennet essence, beaten egg and nutmeg to the milk. Mix well. Either pour the mixture into a 1pt (600ml) decorative bowl or divide between 4 individual dishes.
3. Set in a cool place, but not the refrigerator. Make and eat on same day.

155

Mango Flan

Serves 6

Pastry

6oz (150g) wheatmeal flour

3oz (75g) vegetable fat

3 tblsp cold water

½ grade 4 egg, beaten

Filling

2 large mangoes

juice of 2 limes

4oz (125g) soft brown sugar

2fl oz (50ml) water

1 level tblsp arrowroot

3 tsp water

A tropical flan made with mangoes and limes.

1. To make pastry, sieve flour into a mixing bowl and rub in the fat until the mixture resembles fine breadcrumbs. Add water and mix to a firm dough.

2. Roll out pastry on a floured surface and use to line a 9in (23cm) glass or pottery flan dish. Prick well all over especially where the sides meet the base. Line with kitchen paper and cook, uncovered, on FULL POWER for 6 minutes.

3. Remove from oven and take out kitchen paper. Brush with beaten egg to seal holes. Cook on FULL POWER for a further minute. Leave to cool.

4. Peel the mangoes carefully. Feel where the seed is with the tip of a sharp knife and then cut off 2 slices lengthways down each side of seed. Repeat with the second mango.

5. Cut the mango flesh into ¼in (5mm) thick slices. Put the slices into a shallow bowl and sprinkle over the juice of one lime.

6. Cut the remaining flesh off the mango seeds and transfer the flesh to a 2pt (1.2l) glass or pottery bowl. Add the juice of the second lime, sugar and 2fl oz (50ml) water. Cook, uncovered, on FULL POWER for 5 minutes.

7. Transfer the cooked mango to a food processor or blender and liquidise until smooth.

8. Return to the glass or pottery bowl. Blend the arrowroot to a smooth paste with the remaining water and stir this mixture into the mango pulp.

9. Cook on FULL POWER for 1½ minutes, stirring after every 30 seconds, until the pulp is thick and shiny in appearance. Stir well and allow to cool.

10. Arrange the mango slices in the cooked flan case in a pattern resembling the spokes of a wheel. Then spoon the cooled mango purée over the slices.

Variation

Paw paw flan

Choose the yellow paw paws. Cut in half horizontally and scoop out the pips.

Serves 4

Sauce

2 medium sized lemons

cold water

2oz (50g) golden granulated raw cane syrup

Pudding

2oz (50g) sunflower margarine

4oz (125g) 81% self raising wheatmeal flour

2oz (50g) demerara raw cane sugar

1oz (25g) shelled walnuts, finely chopped

¼pt (150ml) skimmed milk, at room temperature

Lemon Sponge with Lemon Sauce

This is a batter pudding made without eggs. The fresh lemon sauce passes through the batter during cooking giving it a delicious flavour.

1. Squeeze lemon juice into a measuring jug and add water, if necessary, to make up to measure ¼pt (150ml). Stir in sugar briskly and leave to one side until dissolved. Stir from time to time.

2. Meanwhile cook margarine, uncovered, on SIMMER for 1 minute.

3. Mix together flour, sugar and walnuts. Stir in the melted margarine and the milk and beat well to give a smooth batter.

4. Grease a 7in (18cm) deep glass cake dish and pour in the batter.

5. Pour the lemon sauce over the batter then cook, uncovered, on FULL POWER for 15 minutes. Serve immediately.

157

Apricot and Pear Crumble

Serves 6

4 large ripe pears, peeled, cored and chopped

12oz (350g) fresh apricots, halved and stones removed

large pinch cinnamon

3oz (75g) wholemeal flour

1½oz (40g) vegetable fat

1½oz (40g) molasses sugar

1oz (25g) walnuts, chopped

A fragrant autumn crumble made with seasonal pears and apricots. If the fruit is ripe, sugar is unnecessary in the filling.

1. Put pears and apricots into a 2pt (1.2l) pie dish. Sprinkle over a large pinch of cinnamon.
2. Put flour into a small basin and rub in vegetable fat until thoroughly blended. Stir in the sugar and chopped walnuts. Sprinkle over pears and apricots.
3. Cook, uncovered, on FULL POWER for 8 minutes. Brown under a pre-heated conventional grill.
4. Serve fromage frais with the crumble instead of custard.

Mincemeat and Apple Roly Poly

Serves 6

8oz (225g) 85% self raising wheatmeal flour

pinch of salt

4oz (125g) vegetable suet

¼pt (150ml) water

5 level tblsp mincemeat

8oz (225g) cooking apples, peeled, cored and grated

A traditional roly poly using vegetable suet.

1. Tip flour into a 4pt (2.25l) mixing bowl. Sift in salt. Toss in the vegetable suet and add sufficient water to form a soft but not sticky dough.
2. Turn out on to a floured surface and knead lightly.
3. Roll out the pastry into an 11in × 9in (28cm × 23cm) rectangle.

4. Spread the mincemeat over pastry to within 1in (2.5cm) of edges then cover with grated apple.

5. Roll up the pastry like a swiss roll and place on to a 10in (25cm) glass or pottery dish that has been lined with cling film.

6. Cook, uncovered, on FULL POWER for 6½ minutes.

7. Remove from the oven and rest for 5 minutes. Lift the roll out of the dish with the cling film and transfer to a flat plate. Gently lift the cling film away from the base. Cut into slices to serve.

Serves 4

2 medium sized grapefruit

1oz (25g) soya margarine

1oz (25g) dark raw cane sugar

½oz (15g) bran flakes

Crunchy Baked Grapefruit

Here is a very versatile dish — breakfast, a starter for a dinner party or a pudding.

1. Cut the grapefruit in half horizontally. Cut around each segment and place the 4 grapefruit halves into a 10in (25cm) glass or pottery dish.

2. Put the margarine and sugar into a 1pt (600ml) glass or pottery bowl. Cook, uncovered, on FULL POWER for 1 minute. Remove from the oven and stir well.

3. Add the bran flakes to this mixture and stir lightly.

4. Pour 1 tablespoon of the bran flake mixture over each grapefruit half. Cook, uncovered, on FULL POWER for 1½ to 2 minutes.

5. Serve immediately.

159

Christmas Pudding

Each pudding serves 6·8

8oz (225g) sultanas
8oz (225g) seedless raisins
8oz (225g) currants
4oz (125g) mixed peel
6oz (175g) vegetable suet
8oz (225g) soft dark brown sugar
4oz (125g) wholemeal breadcrumbs
4oz (125g) 81% self raising wheatmeal flour
2oz (50g) ground almonds
1 level tsp mixed spice
½ level tsp grated nutmeg
pinch sea salt
3 grade 3 eggs, at room temperature beaten
1 level tblsp black treacle
2fl oz (50ml) brandy
¼pt (150ml) strong dark ale

This is a traditional Christmas pudding and the quantities make two puddings, one for the family and one to give away to relatives or friends. Remember, never put metal charms in the pudding if you cook or reheat it in the microwave.

1. Grease two 2pt (1.2l) glass or pottery pudding basins.
2. Put the dried fruit and mixed peel into a 5pt (2.75l) mixing bowl. Stir in all the dry ingredients.
3. Beat together the eggs and black treacle in a small glass bowl and stir into the fruit. Add the brandy and enough ale to make the mixture soft enough to fall off the wooden stirring spoon or spatula.
4. Divide the mixture between the 2 pudding basins. Cover with cling film and puncture twice with the tip of a knife.
5. Cook each pudding on FULL POWER for 5 minutes. Rest for 5 minutes. Cook again on FULL POWER for 5 minutes.
6. Allow to stand for 5 minutes before turning out of the basin and serving.

To reheat on Christmas Day
Store the Christmas pudding in a cool place, wrapped in foil or cling film. When required, unwrap, return to the glass or pottery basin and cover with fresh cling film. Puncture twice with the tip of a knife. Cook on REHEAT for 5 minutes. Stand for 5 minutes before turning out and serving.

Christmas Pudding
(Photo: The Flour Advisory Bureau)

160

Crème Caramels

Serves 4

2oz (50g) dark raw cane sugar

2 tblsp cold water

1 tblsp boiling water

a little soya margarine

4 grade 3 eggs

1oz (25g) light raw cane sugar

½ tsp vanilla essence

½pt (300ml) low fat single cream

¼pt (150ml) skimmed milk

A popular and traditional dessert, speedily cooked in the microwave.

1. Put the dark cane sugar and cold water into a 1pt (600ml) glass or pottery jug. Cook, uncovered, on FULL POWER for 2 minutes until boiling.

2. Remove from the oven and stir in the boiling water.

3. Divide the syrup between 4 ramekin dishes and tilt the dishes so that the syrup coats the sides. Put the dishes into the refrigerator for a few minutes.

4. When the syrup has set, lightly grease the top part of each ramekin with some soya margarine (the part which is not coated with the caramel).

5. Put the eggs, sugar and vanilla essence into a 4pt (2.25ml) mixing bowl and beat together well.

6. Pour the single cream and skimmed milk into a 2pt (1.2l) glass or pottery bowl. Cook, uncovered, on FULL POWER for 2 minutes until the mixture is about to boil.

7. Pour the hot cream mixture on to the eggs and beat well. Strain into the caramel-lined dishes.

8. Cook, uncovered, on SIMMER for 8 minutes. Remove from the oven and rest for 5 minutes. Turn out when firm and cold.

Cranberry and Apple Mousse (p 166)
(Photo: Ocean Spray Cranberry Sauces & APDC)

Brown Bread and Butter Pudding

Serves 4

6 large slices of wholemeal bread

sufficient soya margarine to spread

3oz (75g) California raisins

1pt (600ml) skimmed milk

2 grade 3 eggs

2oz (50g) light raw cane sugar

A healthy version of an old favourite.

1. Leave the crusts on the bread and spread each slice with soya margarine.
2. Cut each slice into 4 squares. Put half the bread into a greased 2¼pt (1.25l) glass or pottery bowl.
3. Sprinkle on the raisins and top with the remaining bread, margarine sides uppermost.
4. Pour the milk into a 3pt (1.75l) glass or pottery bowl. Cook, uncovered, on FULL POWER for 3 minutes.
5. Remove from the oven and beat in the eggs and sugar. Pour over the bread.
6. Cook, uncovered, on SIMMER for 25 minutes. Remove from the oven and rest for 5 minutes before serving. If liked, brown top under a conventional grill.

Bakewell Tart

Serves 8

6oz (150g) wholemeal flour

3oz (75g) vegetable fat

3 tblsp cold water

½ grade 4 egg, beaten

Filling

4oz (125g) sunflower margarine

4oz (125g) light soft brown sugar

A well-loved, old-fashioned family pudding.

1. To make pastry, sieve flour into a bowl, add fat and rub in finely. Mix to a firm dough with water.
2. Roll out pastry on a floured surface and use to line a 9in (23cm) glass or pottery flan dish. Prick well all over, especially where the sides meet the base. Rest flan for ½ hour in the refrigerator.
3. Line the flan with kitchen paper and cook, uncovered, on FULL POWER for 6 minutes.

2 grade 4 eggs, at room temperature, beaten

2oz (50g) unbleached self raising flour

2oz (50g) ground almonds

3 level tblsp strawberry jam

4. Remove from oven and take out kitchen paper. Brush with the beaten egg to seal the holes. Cook on FULL POWER for a further minute. Leave to cool.

5. Cream together the margarine and sugar until light and fluffy. Beat in the eggs gradually.

6. Sieve flour, add almonds and then fold into creamed mixture.

7. Spread the jam evenly over the base of the cooked flan. Cover smoothly with cake mixture.

8. Cook, uncovered, on SIMMER for 11 minutes.

Home-made Yogurt

1½pt (900ml) silver-topped milk

2 rounded tblsp skimmed milk powder

¼pt (150ml) natural yogurt

An uncomplicated method for making this most versatile food.

1. Heat the milk in the microwave until lukewarm, about 3 to 4 minutes on SIMMER.
2. Whisk in the skimmed milk powder and yogurt.
3. Leave to stand, covered, overnight in a warm place (e.g. near the boiler or in a linen cupboard).
4. When yogurt has set, store in the refrigerator.

Maple Tart

Serves 6-8

Pastry

6oz (175g) malted wheatmeal flour

3oz (75g) vegetable fat

3 tblsp cold water

½ grade 4 egg, beaten

Filling

4oz (125g) bran flakes

6 level tblsp maple syrup

A transatlantic-style tart made with maple syrup.

1. To make pastry, sieve flour into bowl, add fat and rub in finely. Mix to a firm dough with water.
2. Roll out on floured surface and use to line a 9in (23cm) glass or pottery flan dish. Prick well all over, especially where the sides meet the base. Rest flan for ½ hour in the refrigerator.
3. Line the flan with kitchen paper and cook, uncovered, on FULL POWER for 6 minutes.
4. Remove from oven and take out kitchen paper. Brush with the beaten egg to seal the holes. Cook on FULL POWER for a further minute. Leave to cool.
5. Lightly crush bran flakes and stir in the maple syrup.

6. Spoon into flan case. Cook, uncovered, on FULL POWER for 3 minutes. Stand for 2 minutes then cook on FULL POWER for a further 1 minute.
7. Eat warm with cream or ice cream. (As the flan gets colder it gets harder so if you make it earlier in the day, cook on REHEAT for one minute before serving.)

Serves 6

---

3 level tblsp coarse cut marmalade

5oz (150g) 81% wheatmeal self raising flour

½ level tsp baking powder

---

1 level tsp ground ginger

---

pinch sea salt

3oz (75g) soft light brown raw cane sugar

3oz (75g) vegetable suet

---

2 grade 3 eggs, at room temperature, beaten

---

3 tblsp milk

Marmalade Suet Pudding

An ultra-fast cooked pudding with an old-world flavour.

1. Line a 2pt (1.2l) glass or pottery mixing bowl with cling film. Spread the marmalade over the base and set aside temporarily.
2. Put the flour into a large mixing bowl with the baking power, ground ginger, salt and sugar. Mix in the suet evenly, rubbing in with the fingers if necessary to ensure even distribution. (Run your hands under the cold tap to keep them cool.)
3. Add eggs and milk and beat to a smooth batter with a wooden spoon.
4. Spread the batter evenly over the marmalade. Cover with cling film and puncture twice with the tip of a knife.
5. Cook on FULL POWER for 4 minutes. Allow to stand for 3 minutes then remove the cling film.
6. Turn out on to a plate and remove film from the base and sides. Serve with Orange Sauce (page 122).

Cranberry and Apple Mousse

Serves 4 — 6

1lb (500g) Bramley apples, peeled, cored and chopped

185g jar cranberry sauce

1½ tsps gelatine

3 fl oz (75ml) water

5 fl oz (125ml) double cream

3 grade 3 eggs

3oz (75g) caster sugar

The cranberry flavour makes this mousse an unusual and exciting treat.

1. Place the apples into a large bowl and cover with a plate or cling film. Cook on FULL POWER for 6 minutes until soft.

2. Mix apples with cranberry jelly in a blender until smooth.

3. Sprinkle the gelatine on to the water and whisk to blend.

4. Microwave the gelatine on FULL POWER for 30 seconds until steaming. Stir into the apple and cranberry mixture.

5. Whisk the eggs and sugar until thick and creamy, and in a separate bowl whisk the cream to the same consistency. Fold the apple mixture into the eggs and sugar, and then fold in the cream.

6. Pour into a large glass dish, or individual dishes, until set. Decorate with whirls of cream or slices of dessert apple dipped in lemon juice.

PRESERVES

Making preserves in the microwave means fast cooking, better-looking jam or marmalade, more brightly-coloured fruit, and increased flavour. It means no sticky pans to cope with, no burning and minimal evaporation. It means exotic pickles, ketchups and relishes cooked with ease and a cool, steam-free kitchen at the end of it all. Two tips. Firstly, use large glass bowls for cooking chutneys and pickles whenever possible as there is no chemical reaction between glass and vinegar and the mixture will, in consequence, stay clear and bright without a trace of cloud. Secondly, to test jam or marmalade for setting, pour a little of the mixture on to a cold saucer and leave for 2 minutes. If a skin forms on top which wrinkles when touched, setting point is reached. If using a preserving thermometer, it should register 220°F (110°C).

Makes 1 lb (450g)

1 lb (450g) cooking apples
1 oz (25g) mint leaves
⅓ pt (200ml) water
⅓ pt (200ml) white wine vinegar
10 oz (275g) preserving sugar
3 level tblsp finely chopped mint

Mint Jelly

Serve with nut and cereal dishes.

1. Slice the apples 1 in (2.5cm) thick, without peeling or coring, into a 2½pt (1.5l) glass mixing bowl. Add the mint leaves and water. Cover with cling film and puncture twice with the tip of a knife. Cook on FULL POWER for 10 minutes until the apples are reduced to a pulp.

2. Add the vinegar and cook on FULL POWER for 5 minutes. Strain the liquid through a jelly bag for at least 4 hours; preferably overnight. Discard the apple pulp and mint leaves.

3. Rinse out the mixing bowl and measuring jug. Measure the juice back into the mixing bowl; it should be approximately 13fl oz (375ml).

4. Stir the preserving sugar into the liquid.

5. Cook, uncovered, on FULL POWER for 10 minutes, stirring after five minutes to dissolve the sugar.

6. Cook on FULL POWER for 10 minutes and test for setting point.

7. If setting point has not been reached, cook on FULL POWER for a further 5 to 8 minutes, checking at the end of every minute.

8. Remove from cooker. Skim. Stir in the finely chopped mint.

9. Allow the jelly to stand for 2 minutes to cool slightly then stir again to disperse the mint. Pour into warm, sterilised jars.

10. Cover, seal and label in the usual way.

Variations

Crab apple jelly. Use 1 lb (450g) crab apples instead of cooking apples. Omit mint. Serve with vegetable dishes.

Damson jelly. Use 1 lb (450g) damsons instead of apples and again omit the mint. Serve with rice and pasta dishes.

Tip
If you make jellies regularly it's best to buy a jelly bag. However, as a substitute you can use a piece of muslin or a fine handkerchief tied across a bowl.

Strawberry Jam

Makes 1 lb (450g)

1 lemon

1 lb (450g) strawberries

12oz (325g) preserving sugar

A delicious way to remember those delectable summer strawberries.

1. Heat lemon on FULL POWER for 30 seconds to release juice. Squeeze out and measure 2 tablespoons into a 4pt (2.25l) glass or pottery bowl.
2. Rinse strawberries and add them to the bowl of lemon juice. Cook, uncovered, on FULL POWER for 6 minutes until the strawberries are soft.
3. Add sugar and stir until dissolved.
4. Cook, uncovered, on FULL POWER for 5 minutes, remove from oven and stir with a wooden spoon; repeat this process 3 more times and test for setting point.
5. If setting point has not yet been reached, return to oven and cook on FULL POWER for a further 1½ minutes. Test again for setting.
6. Repeat step 5 until setting point is reached.
7. Remove from the cooker and leave to stand until lukewwarm.
8. Stir, then pour into warm, sterilised jars.
9. Cover, seal and label in the usual way.

Makes approx. 3½lb (1.6kg)

1½lb (700g) fruit — about 5 seville oranges and 1 lemon

1pt (575ml) boiling water

1½lb (700g) preserving sugar

Bitter Orange Marmalade

Microwave marmalade uses less sugar than conventional marmalade and has a more fruity taste.

1. Wash fruit then cut in half and remove the pips. Chop the peel and fruit in a food processor or blender.

2. Place the fruit in a 3½pt (2l) glass bowl. Pour over the boiling water and stir with a wooden spoon.

3. Tie the pips in a muslin bag, using a microwave tie or rubber band. Put the bag in the bowl of fruit.

4. Cook, uncovered, on FULL POWER for 5 minutes. Take the bowl out of the cooker, remove the muslin bag, then stir in the sugar until completely dissolved.

5. Return the bowl to the oven and cook on FULL POWER for 20 to 25 minutes until setting point is reached. Stir twice during cooking with a wooden spoon.

6. Remove from cooker and allow to cool until a skin forms. Stir, then pour into warm sterlised jars.

7. Cover, seal and label in the usual way.

Makes approx 1½lb (675g)

Raspberry Jam

*1lb (450g) fresh raspberries,
cleaned*

1lb (450g) preserving sugar

Always a favourite for tea with scones or crumpets.

1. Rinse raspberries and then put into a 4pt (2.25l) glass or pottery bowl. Cook, uncovered, on FULL POWER for 5 minutes until the raspberries are soft.
2. Remove from the microwave and break down by beating with a wooden spoon. Add the sugar and stir until dissolved.
3. Cook, uncovered, on FULL POWER for 5 minutes. Remove from the oven and stir with a wooden spoon.
4. Return bowl to cooker and cook on FULL POWER for a further 5 minutes, then stir well again.
5. Cook on FULL POWER for 2½ minutes and test for setting point.
6. If setting point has not been reached, return to the oven and cook on FULL POWER for further 1½ minutes and test again.
7. Repeat step 6 until setting point is reached.
8. Remove from cooker and leave to stand until lukewarm.
9. Stir, then pour into warm, sterilised jars.
10. Cover, seal and label in the usual way.

Makes about 1½lb (675g)

3 good heads of elderflower,
flowers removed and stalks
discarded

1lb (450g) gooseberries,
topped and tailed

7fl oz (200ml) cold water

1lb (450g) preserving sugar

Gooseberry Jam with Elderflowers

The addition of elderflowers gives this jam a fragrant, countryside taste which sets it apart from ordinary gooseberry jam.

1. Rinse elderflowers. Put them into a 4pt (2.25l) glass or pottery mixing bowl, making sure that no pieces of stem are added.

2. Add the gooseberries and cold water. Cover with cling film and puncture twice with the tip of a knife. Cook on FULL POWER for 5 minutes until gooseberries are soft.

3. Remove from the oven and uncover. Add sugar and stir until dissolved.

4. Cook on FULL POWER for 5 minutes. Remove from oven and stir. Repeat this process 4 more times and then test for setting point.

5. If setting point has not yet been reached, return to the oven and cook on FULL POWER for a further 1½ minutes. Test again for setting point.

6. Repeat step 5 until setting point is reached.

7. Remove from cooker and leave to stand until lukewarm.

8. Stir, then pour into warm sterlised jars.

9. Cover, seal and label in the usual way.

Corn Relish

Makes 3lb (1.5kg)

4 corn on the cobs

¼pt (150ml) cold water

1lb (450g) green cabbage, coarsely chopped

8oz (225g) green pepper, de-seeded and coarsely chopped

4oz (125g) onion, quartered

¼ level tsp turmeric

1 level tsp sea salt

½ level tsp powdered mustard

½pt (300ml) cider vinegar

4oz (125g) raw cane granulated sugar

A sunshine pickle which is tantalisingly sweet-sour. Serve it with egg and nut dishes.

1. Put the sweetcorn cobs into a shallow dish with the water. Cover with cling film and puncture twice with the tip of a knife. Cook on FULL POWER for 10 minutes, remove from oven and allow to stand for 5 minutes.

2. Finely chop the cabbage, pepper and onion in a food processor or blender. Put into a 4pt (2.25l) glass or pottery bowl and set aside temporarily.

3. Put the turmeric, salt, mustard, vinegar and sugar into a 2pt (1.2l) glass or pottery bowl. Cover with cling film and puncture twice with the tip of a knife. Cook on FULL POWER for 2½ minutes. Carefully fold back the cling film and stir vinegar to dissolve the sugar. Re-cover and cook on FULL POWER for further 2½ minutes. Uncover and stir vinegar again. Cook, uncovered, on FULL POWER for further 5 minutes.

4. Cut the kernels off the sweetcorn cobs with a knife. Stir into the cabbage mixture.

5. Add the vinegar and stir well. Cook, uncovered, on FULL POWER for 20 minutes, stirring after each 5 minutes.

6. Put the pickle into clean, sterilised jars, then seal and label in the usual way.

Glass bowls best for chutneys as no reaction by chemical as with saucepans, etc. & clearer colour.

Mixed Vegetable Chutney

Makes 2lb (900g)

8oz (225g) tomatoes, peeled and chopped
8oz (225g) cup mushrooms, sliced
¼pt (150ml) wine vinegar
4oz (125g) green pepper, de-seeded and chopped
4oz (125g) onion, finely chopped
8oz (225g) cooking apples, peeled and finely chopped
1 clove garlic, crushed
6oz (175g) soft light brown sugar

A fine-flavoured chutney, designed for curry and egg dishes.

1. Put tomatoes and mushrooms into a 3pt (1.75l) glass mixing bowl. Pour over half the vinegar.
2. Stir in green pepper, onion, apples and garlic. Cover with cling film and puncture twice with the tip of a knife.
3. Cook on FULL POWER for 5 minutes. Stir, re-cover and cook on FULL POWER for a further 5 minutes.
4. Stir in the remaining vinegar and sugar and cook, uncovered, on FULL POWER for 5 minutes or until chutney thickens.
5. Spoon into warm sterilised jars. Label and seal.

Spiced Red Cabbage

Makes 3lb

½ red cabbage (1¼lb/500g)
1lb (450g) cooking apples
8.8fl oz (250ml) bottle of lemon and black pepper vinegar or white wine vinegar
grated rind and juice of 1 small orange
2oz (50g) soft brown sugar

Be careful! When you transfer the cooked cabbage to the jars, put the jars on a thick layer of newspaper — purple vinegar can stain your clothes.

1. Shred the red cabbage into a 5pt (2.75l) bowl. Peel, core and slice the apples into the same bowl then pour on the vinegar.
2. Add the grated rind and juice from the orange and stir well to blend the ingredients.

3. Cover bowl with cling film and puncture twice with the tip of a knife. Cook on FULL POWER for 10 minutes.

4. Remove from the microwave and stir sugar into the cabbage mixture with a wooden spoon.

5. Return to the microwave, and cook, uncovered, on FULL POWER for 5 minutes. Stir.

6. Carefully spoon the red cabbage into warm clean jars. Allow to cool then put lids on the jars.

Makes about ¾pt (400ml)

1lb (450g) open mushrooms

½oz (15g) sea salt

½ tsp black peppercorns

½ tsp whole allspice

---

5 cloves

1in (2.5cm) piece root ginger, peeled

½pt (300ml) white wine vinegar

Mushroom Ketchup

A Victorian-style ketchup which goes well with savoury pies and flans.

1. Wipe the mushrooms, cut into fairly large pieces and place in a 3pt (1.75l) bowl. Sprinkle over the salt and mix well. Cover with a plate and leave overnight.

2. Next day, rinse the mushrooms and drain well. Chop finely in a blender or food processor and put into a 3pt (1.75l) glass or pottery bowl.

3. Crush peppercorns, allspice and cloves and finely grate the root ginger. Add to mushroom mixture with vinegar. Mix well.

4. Cook on FULL POWER for 10 minutes, remove from the oven and stir. Cook on FULL POWER for a further 10 minutes.

5. Stir round and allow to stand for 5 minutes.

6. Purée the mushroom mixture in a blender of food processor and pour into warm, sterilised jars or bottles. Seal and label in the usual way.

Makes approx 2lb (1kg)

½pt (300ml) white wine vinegar
2 level tsp pickling spice
1lb (450g) red peppers, de-seeded and coarsely chopped
1lb (450g) green peppers, de-seeded and coarsely chopped
2pt (1.2l) cold water
1lb (450g) onions, quartered
½ level tsp sea salt
4oz (125g) raw cane granulated sugar

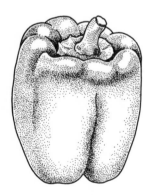

Green and Red Pepper Pickle

A colourful pickle, ideal for barbecues in the summer.

1. Put vinegar and spice into a 2pt (1.2l) glass or pottery bowl. Cover with cling film and puncture twice with the tip of a knife. Cook on FULL POWER for 6 minutes.

2. Remove from the oven and leave until cold. Strain the vinegar into a jug to remove the spices and set aside temporarily.

3. Put peppers into a 4pt (2.25l) glass or pottery bowl and cover with half the water. Cover with cling film and puncture twice with the tip of a knife. Cook on FULL POWER for 5 minutes. Drain the peppers.

4. Return to the bowl and add remaining water. Re-cover and cook on FULL POWER for 5 minutes. Drain.

5. Put half the spiced vinegar and the onions into a blender or food processor and chop coarsely. Put into a 4pt (2.25l) glass or pottery bowl and set aside.

6. Put the remaining vinegar and the blanched peppers into a blender or food processor and chop coarsely then add them to the onion mixture and mix well.

7. Stir in the salt and sugar. Cook, uncovered, on FULL POWER for 20 minutes, stirring every 5 minutes, until mixture has thickened.

8. Pour into hot, clean jars. Seal and label in the usual way.

Preserves
(Photo: TI Creda)

HOME MADE
Green & Red Pepper Pickle
HOME MADE
Corn Relish
HOME MADE
Strawberry Jam
Creda
HOME MADE
Gooseberry

DRINKS

Punches, Cups, Nightcaps and Toddies add up to a
cheerful selection of drinks for any time of year.
Even a Wassail Bowl has been included for the
merriment of Christmas guests.

Apricot and Peach Cup (p 179) with
Mixed Nut Pâté (p 46)
(Photo: TI Creda)

Almond Punch

2 lemons

8oz (225g) light raw cane sugar

¼ level tsp ground ginger

1pt (600ml) water

½pt (300ml) strong tea

½pt (300ml) pineapple juice

1 tsp vanilla essence

1 tsp almond essence

1pt (600ml) ginger ale

A long, cool non-alcoholic punch.

1. Wash and dry lemons and grate off peel. Cook whole lemons on FULL POWER for 30 seconds to release the juice. Cut each in half, squeeze out the juice and reserve. Discard pithy shells. Reserve juice.

2. Put sugar, ginger, water, and chopped lemon peel in a 3pt (1.75l) glass or pottery bowl. Cook on FULL POWER, uncovered, for 8 minutes, stirring twice. Allow to cool.

3. Make tea in the conventional way and leave to cool.

4. Strain the lemon peel and ginger syrup into a 5pt (2.75l) jug or punch bowl.

5. Strain the cooled tea and add.

6. Pour the pineapple juice, lemon juice and essences into the jug or punch bowl and stir well to blend. Chill.

7. When ready to serve, add ginger ale.

Tip
For a variation, add 2oz (50g) creamed coconut at step 2 and reduce almond essence to ¼ teaspoon Omit vanilla essence.

Milk and Cider Nightcap

Serves 1

¼pt (150ml) whole milk

1 grade 4 egg

1 level tsp clear honey

2 tblsp medium sweet cider

Warm and sweet for cold winter's evenings.

1. Pour milk into a 1pt (600ml) glass or pottery jug. Beat in the egg and honey.

2. Cook on ROAST for 2 minutes until just beginning to thicken.

3. Remove from oven and beat very well.

4. Add cider, beating continuously.

5. Serve in a warm mug.

Apricot and Peach Cup

Makes about 4pt (2.25l)

8oz (225g) fresh apricots, halved and stones removed

½pt (300ml) water

2 level tblsp maple syrup

8oz (225g) fresh peaches, skinned and finely chopped

½pt (300ml) fresh apple juice

2in (5cm) piece of cinnamon stick

1 x 730ml bottle sparkling cider

1 banana, peeled and sliced

A glorious fruit punch to take the heat out of scorching summer days.

1. Put apricot halves and water into a 1pt (600ml) glass or pottery bowl. Cover with cling film and puncture twice with the tip of a knife. Cook on FULL POWER for 3 minutes until the fruit is soft.

2. Purée in a blender or food processor. Transfer pulp to a 3pt (1.75l) jug or punch bowl. Add the maple syrup and chopped peaches. Stir well.

3. Pour apple juice into a 1pt (600ml) glass or pottery bowl. Add the cinnamon stick. Cover with cling film as before and cook on FULL POWER for 3 minutes to infuse, then remove from the microwave and cool.

4. Remove cinnamon stick and add the apple juice to the fruit mixture. Stir well and chill.

5. Just before serving, pour the sparkling cider into the fruit mixture and stir well. Float the banana slices on top and serve in tall glasses.

Warm Grapefruit Cup

Makes approximately 2½pt (1.5l)

1 large grapefruit
½pt (300ml) tea
2oz (50g) dark raw cane sugar
1 x 35.2fl oz (1l) bottle of sweet cider
2 tblsp brandy

A marvellous hot punch for cold winter's evenings, especially when grapefruits are in season.

1. Pare approximately half the rind from the grapefruit with a potato peeler. Put into a small bowl. Cover with boiling water and allow to stand for 2 minutes. Strain. Cut into thin strips and set aside for decoration.
2. Place the whole grapefruit into the microwave and cook on FULL POWER for 30 seconds to release the juice. Squeeze out.
3. Put into a 5pt (2.75l) glass or pottery bowl with remaining ingredients. Cover with cling film and puncture twice with the tip of a knife.
4. Cook on FULL POWER for 6½ minutes until warm but not boiling.
5. Serve in cups with the strips of grapefruit rind for decoration.

Raspberry Fruit Cup

Makes 2½pt (1.5l)

8oz (225g) fresh raspberries
1 x 70cl bottle rosé wine
6 tblsp dark raw cane sugar
2in (5cm) piece of cinnamon stick
grated rind of half an orange

Raspberries and rosé wine are perfectly matched in this elegant fruit cup, unusually served hot.

1. Purée raspberries in a blender or food processor with half the wine.
2. Strain (to remove raspberry pips) into a 4pt (2.25l) glass or pottery bowl.

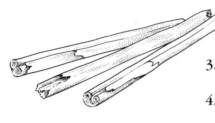

3. Add the sugar, the rest of the wine and the cinnamon stick. Stir well.

4. Cover with cling film and puncture twice with the tip of a knife. Heat on FULL POWER for 4½ minutes until hot but not boiling. Stir once during cooking.

5. Stir in the grated orange rind and serve in warmed cups.

Hot Cocoa/Carob Drink

The perfect drink for relaxation before bedtime.

Serves 1

1 to 1½ level tsp cocoa or carob

1 to 1½ tsp cold skimmed milk

½oz (15g) plain chocolate or carob bar

¼pt (150ml) skimmed milk

2 white marshmallows

1. Put cocoa or carob powder into a 1pt (600ml) glass or pottery jug and blend with the 1 to 1½ teaspoons milk.

2. Into this, break the ½oz (15g) chocolate or carob bar. Cover with cling film and puncture twice with the tip of a knife.

3. Cook on FULL POWER for 30 seconds.

4. Remove the cling film and whisk in the remaining milk.

5. Cook, uncovered, on FULL POWER for a further minute.

6. Remove from the oven and stir well. Gently drop in the white marshmallows and cook, uncovered, on FULL POWER for further 15 seconds.

7 To serve, pour into a mug and stir gently.

Makes 2¼pts (1.25l)

½pt (300ml) water

---

2 cinnamon sticks, each 3in (7.5cm) long

---

pinch freshly grated nutmeg

---

6 whole cloves

2oz (50g) light raw cane sugar

---

grated rind and juice of 1 lemon

---

1 x 70cl bottle English apple wine or apple juice if non-alcholic drink is preferred

---

1 unpeeled red dessert apple, cored and sliced into rings

Spiced Apple Punch

An almost perfumed punch for winter pleasure with apple ring 'floats'.

1. Put water, cinnamon sticks, nutmeg, cloves, sugar and lemon rind into a 1½pt (900ml) glass or pottery bowl. Cover with cling film and puncture twice with the tip of a knife. Cook on FULL POWER for 4 minutes. Uncover, stir and re-cover. Cook again on FULL POWER for further 1 minute.

2. Strain liquid into a 3pt (1.75l) glass or pottery bowl. Add the lemon juice and apple wine or juice.

3. Cook, uncovered, on FULL POWER for 4 minutes.

4. Serve hot, with the apple slices floating on the top.

Makes approx 2 pts (1.2l)

¼pt (150ml) water

---

2 to 3 level tblsp honey

---

pared rind of 1 lemon

2in (5cm) piece of cinnamon stick

---

2 small oranges stuck with 15 whole cloves

---

1 x 70cl bottle red wine

2½fl oz (65ml) brandy

Red Wine Punch

A hearty, traditional punch for winter parties.

1. Put the water, honey, lemon rind, cinnamon stick and oranges stuck with cloves into a 3pt (1.75l) glass or pottery bowl. Heat on FULL POWER for 3 minutes.

2. Remove from the oven and stir well. Return to the oven and continue cooking on FULL POWER for a further 2 minutes.

3. Lift lemon rind and oranges out of the punch syrup. Add the red wine and brandy.

4. Cover the bowl with cling film and puncture twice with the tip of a knife. Heat on FULL POWER for 6½ minutes until hot but not quite boiling.
5. Ladle into warm cups to serve.

Hot Rum Punch

Makes about 2pt (1.2l)

8oz (225g) fresh blackcurrants

½pt (300ml) tea, made in the conventional way and strained

½ level tsp ground cinnamon

4 level tblsp maple syrup

2oz (50g) soft brown sugar

¾pt (450ml) red wine

7fl oz (200ml) dark rum

The vitamin 'C' from the blackcurrants is a good excuse to enjoy this warming punch.

1. Put the blackcurrants, tea and cinnamon into a 2pt (1.2l) glass or pottery bowl. Cover with cling film and puncture twice with the tip of a knife. Cook on FULL POWER for 4 minutes.
2. In a food processor or blender, purée the blackcurrant mixture.
3. Sieve the purée into a 3pt (1.75l) glass or pottery bowl using a fine metal sieve. Add the maple syrup and sugar. Stir well to dissolve the sugar.
4. Pour in the wine and the rum.
5. Cover with cling film and puncture twice with the tip of a knife. Cook on FULL POWER for 5 minutes until hot but not boiling.
6. Serve in warmed mugs.

183

Wassail Bowl

Makes 2¼pt (1.25l)

2pts (1.2l) good ale

¼pt (150ml) sweet sherry

¼ level tsp ground cinnamon

¼ level tsp ground ginger

¼ level tsp freshly-grated
nutmeg

2 strips of lemon rind

2 green dessert apples

2 level tblsp soft dark brown
sugar

Here is a traditional Wassail bowl from the hop growing county of Kent. In the west country or Herefordshire, cider is used instead of ale.

1. Put ale, sherry, spices and lemon rind into a 3pt (1.75l) glass or pottery bowl. Cover with cling film and puncture twice with the tip of a knife. Cook on FULL POWER for 4 minutes.
2. Quarter and core apples.
3. Add the apples to the ale mixture then stir in the sugar.
4. Re-cover with cling film and puncture twice with the tip of a knife. Cook on FULL POWER for a further 4 to 5 minutes until very hot and apples partly baked.
5. Ladle into mugs to serve.

Hot Toddy

Serves 4

1¼pt (750ml) skimmed milk

2½fl oz (65ml) whisky

2 level tblsp clear honey

2 grade 3 eggs, beaten

1 level tsp freshly-grated
nutmeg

A traditional winter warmer; one of the best things to come home to after a busy day.

1. Put milk, whisky and honey into a 2pt (1.2l) glass or pottery jug or bowl. Cook on FULL POWER for 4 minutes, stirring half way through.
2. Add the beaten eggs, stir round and strain mixture into 4 warmed, heatproof tumblers.
3. Sprinkle with the grated nutmeg and serve straight away.

_MISCELLANEOUS

Practical snippets for you to follow include
toasting nuts, melting chocolate, warming milk
and drying breadcrumbs, herbs and chillies.

Drying Herbs

The microwave is a real bonus if you have fresh herbs to dry. They keep a superb green colour and dry surprisingly fast.

Basil

Place 1oz (25g) basil leaves on to a double layer of kitchen paper placed either on a plate or directly on to the turntable. Make sure the leaves are evenly distributed and there are no large stalks. Heat on FULL POWER for 3 minutes, until the leaves are bright green and thoroughly dried (they should sound like autumn leaves when rustled). Move the leaves around on the kitchen paper after every minute. Crush between palms of hands and store in an airtight container.

Bay Leaves

As for basil but do not crush the leaves.

Coriander

This herb is very useful to dry as it can be difficult to purchase and is awkward to grow. Dry in the same way as basil, but when the leaves have been crushed, put them back into the microwave and cook on FULL POWER for 1 minute more to ensure that any pieces of stem have been dried. It is impossible to remove all the stems when sorting out the leaves.

Mint

Follow instructions for basil but if the leaves are large, cook on SIMMER.

Rosemary

Follow instructions for basil but cook on FULL POWER for 2 minutes. Do not crush the leaves.

Toasting Nuts

To toast 2oz (50g) hazelnuts

Put whole hazlenuts on a glass or pottery plate. Cook, uncovered, on FULL POWER for 11 minutes, removing the plate and moving the kernels with a fork after every 1½ minutes. Leave to cool on the plate to allow for further slow cooking and to ensure crispness. Rub off skins when cold.

To toast 2oz (50g) blanched almonds

Cook, uncovered, on FULL POWER for 7 to 8 minutes or until light golden brown in colour.

Again remove plate and stir nuts every 1½ minutes. This method can also be used for *cashew nuts.*

Again remove plate and stir nuts each 1½ minutes. This method can also be used for *cashew nuts.*

To toast 2oz (50g) coconut

Cook desiccated coconut, uncovered, on FULL POWER for 5 minutes. To cook shredded coconut, cook for 6 minutes.

To toast 1lb (450g) peanuts

Spread shelled peanuts over the base of a glass or pottery shallow-sided dish. Cook, uncovered, on FULL POWER for 15 to 17 minutes removing the plate and turning the nuts after every 5 minutes to ensure even browning. When cool, rub any loose or browned skin off the nuts between the palms of hands.

INDEX

Almond(s), Punch 178
  Walnut and, Nuggets
    47
Apple(s)
  and Berry Meringue
    Flan 154
  and Nut Stuffing Balls
    46
  Baked Stuffed 150
  Brown Betty 150
  Cider, Cheese and,
    Sauce 120
  Cranberry and, Mousse
    166
  Lentil and, Loaf 34
  Mincemeat and, Roly
    Poly 158
  Red Lentil and, Pâté 20
  Shredded Red Cabbage
    and Bramley 86
  Spiced, Punch 182
Apricot(s)
  and Date Crunch
    Wedges 142
  and Peach Cup 179
  and Pear Crumble 158
  Nutty, Cake 143
Asparagus and Cheese
  Flan 78
Aubergine(s)
  Lemony Chick Pea and,
    Casserole with
    Sesame Dumplings
    28
  Stuffed 81
Avocado(es)
  and Tomato Flan 88
  Curried, and Port 82
  Hot, with Nutty
    Mushroom Stuffing
    91

Baked Jacket Potatoes
  100
Baked Okra 98
Baked Pawpaw 95
Baked Plantain 87
Baked Stuffed Apples 150
Bakewell Tart 162
Balkan Tomato Sauce 118
Banana(s)
  and Raspberry Baked
    Custard 152
  Bread 142
  Caribbean 152
Barbecue Sauce 120
Beansprout(s)
  Cheese and, Loaf 67
Beetroot
  and Orange Soup 12
  Courgette, Baby Beet
    and Tomato
    Crumble 89
  with Shredded Red
    Cabbage 82
Bitter Orange Marmalade
  170
Black Bean(s)
  Crusty-Topped
    Casserole 33
Blackberry(ies)
  Orange and, Lattice
    Flan 151
Braised Vegetables 106
Brandy Snaps 138
Breadcrumbs, Drying 189
Brown Bread and Butter
  Pudding 162
Buttermilk Scones 136

Cabbage
  Beetroot with
    Shredded Red 82

Creamy Eggs baked in
  70
Parsley and Lemon 79
Shredded Red, with
  Bramley Apples 86
Spiced Red 174
Stuffed 84
Caerphilly and Nut
  Stuffed Peppers 107
Cannellini with French
  Beans and Salad 36
Cannelloni with
  Vegetable Nut Stuffing
  54
Caper Sauce 114
Caribbean Bananas 152
Carrot(s)
  and Coriander Soup 11
Cake 134
  Cheese and, Pie with
    Wholemeal Pastry 71
Cauliflower
  and Tomato Mozarella
    Flan 90
  Curried, and Beans 83
  Polonaise 80
Celery
  Chestnut and, Cake 45
  Chicory with, and Red
    Leicester Sauce 96
Cheese Dishes
  and Beansprout Loaf 67
  and Carrot Pie with
    Wholemeal Pastry 71
  and Potato Layer Pie 72
  and Rice Salad 51
  Caerphilly and Nut
    Stuffed Peppers 107
  Caraway Bread 130
  Cauliflower and
    Tomato Mozarella

Flan 90
Cheesy Vegetable
    Lasagne 57
Chicory with Celery
    and Red Leicester
    Sauce 96
Cider, and Apple Sauce
    120
Courgette and Gruyère
    Cheese Puff 86
Curried, Tart 76
Fondue 72
Layered Ratatouille and
    Dolcelatte 104
Lentil and, Soup 12
Noodles with
    Caerphilly Cheese
    and Onions 63
Noodles with
    Wenslydale Cheese,
    Tomatoes and Garlic
    60
Nutty Mushroom and
    Stilton Pie 74
Tagliatelli with Creamy
    Walnut and, Sauce
    53
Cheesy Vegetable Lasagne
    57
Chestnut and Celery Cake
    45
Chick Pea(s)
    Lemony, and Aubergine
    Casserole with
    Sesame Dumplings
    28
Chicory with Celery and
    Red Leicester Sauce 96
Chilled Lettuce and
    Cucumber Sauce 15
Chilli Bean Stuffed Dutch
    Tomatoes 108
Chilli Lentil and
    Mushroom Pie 22
Chillies, Drying 187
Chinese-Style Rice and
    Egg Scramble with
    Vegetables 62
Chocolate
    Melting 187
    Truffles 148

Christmas Cake 133
Christmas Pudding 160
Chutney, Mixed
    Vegetable 174
Cider
    Cheese and Apple
    Sauce 120
    Country Vegetable
    Hotpot with 108
    Milk and, Night cap
    178
    Cocoa/Carob Drink,
    Hot 181
Corn
    Leek with, Soup 10
    Relish 173
Country Vegetable Hot
    Pot with Cider 108
Courgette(s)
    and Gruyère Cheese
    Puff 86
    Baby Beet and Tomato
    Crumble 89
    Mange Tout and
    Tomato Tart 85
Couscous with Bulgar
    Wheat 24
Cranberry(ies)
    and Apple Mousse 166
    and Orange Sauce 124
Creamy Eggs baked in
    Cabbage 70
Creamy Kidney Bean
    Wholewheat Pancakes
    30
Creme Caramels 161
Crumbed Potatoes with
    Parmesan and Chives
    93
Crunchy Baked
    Grapefruit 159
Crunchy Lentil Balls 23
Crusty Topped Black
    Bean Casserole 33
Cucumber
    and Watercress Soup
    14
    Chilled Lettuce and, Soup
    15
Cumberland Sauce 119
Curried Avocado and Port

82
Curried Cauliflower and
    Beans 83
Curried Cheese Tart 76
Curried Vegetable Risotto
    50

Date(s)
    Apricot and, Crunch
    Wedges 142
    Tea Bread 139
Devilled Black-eyed Bean
    Casserole 25
Drying Herbs 186

Egg Dishes
    and Leek Bake 68
    and Lentil Curry 69
    Chinese-Style Rice and,
    Scramble with
    Vegetables 62
    Creamy, baked in
    Cabbage 70
    Custard Sauce 124
    Florentine 66
    Fluffy Spinach
    Omelette 75
    Savoury, and Parsley
    Crumble 73
    Scrambled 66

Fig Loaf 146
Fluffy Spinach Omelette
    75
French Bean(s)
    Cannellini with, and
    Salad 36
Fruit Compôte 155
Fruit Loaf 138

Gingerbread 136
Gnocchi 35
Gooseberry Jam with
    Elderflowers 172
Granary and Spring
    Onion Scones 137
Grapefruit

Crunchy Baked 159
Warm, Cup 180
Green and Red Pepper
Pickle 176
Green Pea Rissoles 31

Hazelnut, Garlic and
Rosemary Loaf 40
Herb(s), Drying 186
Hollandaise Sauce 116
Home-made Yogurt 164
Honey and Carob Cake
145
Horseshoe Plait 132
Hot Avocado with Nutty
Mushroom Stuffing 91
Hot Cocoa/Carob Drink
181
Hot Cross Buns 144
Hot Rum Punch 183

Indian Spice Rice 61

Jerusalem Artichoke Soup
with Nutmeg 18
Junket, Spiced 155

Kidney Bean(s)
Creamy, Wholewheat
Pancakes 30
Red Bean Curry 26
Red, Dip, à la
Guacamole 32

Layered Ratatouille and
Dolcelatte 104
Leek(s)
Egg and, Bake 68
with Corn Soup 10
Lemon Sponge with
Lemon Sauce 157
Lemony Chick Pea and
Aubergine Casserole
with Sesame
Dumplings 28
Lemony Wheat with

Brazils and Peanuts 40
Lentil(s)
and Apple Loaf 34
and Cheese Soup 12
and Tomato Soup 16
Chilli, and Mushroom
Pie 22
Crunchy, Balls 73
Egg and, Curry 69
Mixed, Lasagne 52
Parsnip and, Crumble
29
Red, and Apple Pâté 20
Red, and Tomato Soup
16
Salad 21
Spaghetti with Spicy 56
Lettuce
Chilled, and Cucumber
Soup 15
Low Fat Mayonnaise
without Oil 115

Macaroni and Flageolet
Supper 55
Mange Tout
Courgette, and Tomato
Tart 85
Mango Flan 156
Maple Tart 164
Marmalade
and Ginger Sauce 123
Bitter Orange 170
Suet Pudding 165
Mayonnaise, Low Fat
without Oil 115
Milk
and Cider Nightcap
178
Mincemeat and Apple
Roly Poly 158
Minestrone Soup 17
Mint Jelly 168
Mixed Lentil Lasagne 52
Mixed Nut Pâté 46
Mixed Nut Rolls with
Cheese Pastry 38
Mixed Pepper and
Pumpkin Ramekins 94
Mixed Vegetable and

Herb Cake 105
Mixed Vegetable
Casserole with Nut
Dumplings 43
Mixed Vegetable Chutney
174
Mixed Vegetables with
Horseradish Crumble
103
Mushroom(s)
and Nut Meat Pudding
44
and Potato Wedges 98
Chilli Lentil and, Pie 22
Hot Avocado with
Nutty, Stuffing 91
Ketchup 175
Nutty, and Stilton Pie
74
Sauce 114
Soup 13
Stuffed, with Sunflower
Seeds 97

Noodles
with Caerphilly Cheese
and Onions 63
with Wensleydale
Cheese,
Tomatoes and Garlic
60
Nutmeg Sauce 115
Nut Dishes
Apple and, Stuffing
Balls 46
Caerphilly and, Stuffed
Peppers 107
Cannelloni with
Vegetable, Stuffing
54
Chestnut and Celery
Cake 45
Hazelnut, Garlic and
Rosemary Loaf 40
Hot Avocado with
Nutty Mushroom
Stuffing 91
Lemony Wheat with
Brazils and Peanuts
40

Mixed, Pâté 46
Mixed, Rolls with
  Cheese pastry 38
Mixed Vegetable
  Casserole with,
  Dumplings 43
Mushroom and Nut
  Meat Pudding 44
Nutty Apricot Cake
  143
Nutty Mushroom and
  Stilton Pie 74
Sweet Fruit and,
  Risotto 58
Sweet 'n' Sour Tofu and
  Cashew Casserole 48
Tagliatelli with Creamy
  Walnut and Cheese
  Sauce 53
Toasting 188
Tomato and Cashew
  Nut Savoury Rice 54
Walnut and Almond
  Nuggets 47
Walnut and Potato Pie
  39
White Nut and
  Horseradish Ring 42
White Nut Cutlets with
  Cheese and Herbs 42
Nutty Apricot Cake 143
Nutty Mushroom and
  Stilton Pie 74

Okra, Baked 98
Onions, Stuffed 105
Orange(s)
  and Blackberry Lattice
  Flan 151
  Beetroot and, Soup 12
  Bitter, Marmalade 170
  Bran Cake 147
  Cranberry and, Sauce
  124
  Sauce 122

Parsley and Lemon
  Cabbage 79
Parsnip(s)
  and Lentil Crumble 29

Cake 134
Pawpaw, Baked 95
Pea(s)
  Green, Rissoles 31
Peach(es)
  Apricot and, Cup 179
Pear(s)
  Apricot and, Crumble
  158
Pepper(s)
  Caerphilly and Nut
  Stuffed, 107
  Green and Red, Pickle
  176
  Mixed, and Pumpkin
  Ramekins 94
  Pickle and Pineapple
  Sauce 117
Pineapple
  and Cider Sauce 125
  Pepper, Pickle and,
  Sauce 117
Plantain, Baked 87
Porridge 20
Potato(es)
  and Runner Bean Bake
  94
  Baked Jacket 100
  Cheese and, Layer Pie
  72
  Crumbed, with
  Parmesan and Chives
  93
  Mushroom and,
  Wedges 98
  Pizza Flan 92
  Pots 101
  Swiss-Style Rösti 92
  Walnut and, Pie 39
Pumpkin
  Mixed Pepper and,
  Ramekins 94
Punch
  Almond 178
  Hot Rum 183
  Red Wine 182
  Spiced Apple 182
Puréed Fruits 126

Raspberry(ies)
  Banana and, Baked

Custard 152
Fruit Cup 180
Jam 171
Red Bean Curry 26
Red Kidney Bean Dip, à la
  Guacamole 32
Red Lentil(s)
  and Apple Pâté 20
  and Tomato Soup 16
Red Wine Punch 182
Rhubarb and Raisin Flan
  153
Rice Dishes
  and Beans 60
  Cheese and, Salad 51
  Chinese-Style, and Egg
  Scramble with
  Vegetables 62
  Curried Vegetable
  Risotto 50
  Indian Spice 61
  Sweet Fruit and Nut
  Risotto 58
  Tomato and Cashew
  Nut Savoury 54
  with Mung Beans and
  Coconut Milk 64
Rye Bread with Herbs
  129

Savoury Egg and Parsley
  Crumble 73
Scone(s)
  Buttermilk 136
  Granary and Spring
  Onion 137
Scottish Black Bun 141
Scrambled Eggs 66
Shredded Red Cabbage
  with Bramley Apples
  86
Simnel Cake 140
Spaghetti with Spicy
  Lentils 56
Spiced Apple Punch 182
Spiced Junket 155
Spiced Red Cabbage 174
Spicy Root Vegetable
  Curry 102
Spinach

Fluffy, Omelette 75
Split Pea Soup 10
Spring Vegetable Medley 111
Stir-Fry Chinese Leaves 99
Strawberry Jam 169
Strong Mustard Sauce 122
Stuffed Aubergines 81
Stuffed Mushrooms with Sunflower Seeds 97
Stuffed Onions 105
Sweet and Sour Sauce 116
Sweet Fruit and Nut Risotto 58
Sweet 'n' Sour Tofu and Cashew Casserole 48
Sweet Potato Soup 14

Tagliatelli with Creamy Walnut and Cheese Sauce 53
Toasting Nuts 187
Tofu
    Sweet 'n' Sour, and Cashew Casserole 48

with Flageolet Beans 27
Tomatoe(es)
    and Cashew Nut Savoury Rice 54
    Avocade and, Flan 88
    Balkan, Sauce 118
    Cauliflower and, Mozarella Flan 90
    Cheese and, Macaroni Casserole 59
    Chilli Bean Stuffed Dutch 108
    Courgette, Baby Beet and, Crumble 89
    Courgette, Mange Tout and, Tart 85
    Noodles with Wensleydale Cheese, and Garlic 60
    Red Lentil and, Soup 16

Vegetable Cobbler with Wholemeal Scone Topping 110
Vegetable Moussaka 112

Vegetable Pâté 106
Vegetarian Kebabs 109

Walnut(s)
    and Almond Nuggets 47
    and Potato Pie 39
    Tagliatelli with Creamy, and Cheese Sauce 53
Warm Grapefruit Cup 180
Wassail Bowl 184
Watercress
    Cucumber and, Soup 14
Wheatmeal Loaf 128
Wheatmeal Madeira Cake 146
White Nut and Horseradish Ring 42
White Nut Cutlets with Cheese and Herbs 42
White Sauce 114

Yogurt
    Home-made 164